Songs of the Baka and
and
Other Discoveries

Travels after Sixty-Five

DENNIS JAMES

PHOTOGRAPHY BY BARBARA GROSSMAN

Skyhorse Publishing

Copyright © 2017 by Dennis James

Skyhorse Publishing books may be purchased in bulk at special discounts for sales promotion, corporate gifts, fund-raising, or educational purposes. Special editions can also be created to specifications. For details, contact the Special Sales Department, Skyhorse Publishing, 307 West 36th Street, 11th Floor, New York, NY 10018 or info@skyhorsepublishing.com.

Skyhorse® and Skyhorse Publishing® are registered trademarks of Skyhorse Publishing, Inc.®, a Delaware corporation.

Visit our website at www.skyhorsepublishing.com.

10 9 8 7 6 5 4 3 2 1

Library of Congress Cataloging-in-Publication Data is available on file.

"Algeria: Blood, Sand, and Natural Gas" first appeared in the Legal Studies Forum under the title "Algeria Journal."

"Cuba: State of the Arts" first appeared in the North American Congress on Latin America (NACLA) Report on the Americas.

Cover design by Anthony Morais
Cover photo credit by Barbara Grossman

Print ISBN: 978-1-5107-1350-5
Ebook ISBN: 978-1-5107-1352-9

Printed in the United States of America

Dedication

To all the people who welcomed us,
into their countries, into their villages,
and into their homes.

"One's destination is never a place,
but a new way of seeing things." —Henry Miller

"When you come to a fork in the road,
take it." —Yogi Berra

Contents

Introduction

Barbara Grossman and I spent our professional lives practicing law in Detroit, Michigan. We met in 1997, married in 2001, and retired and moved to New York City in 2005.

Among our many common interests is a desire to travel. Raising children during a prior marriage and practicing law as a partner in a small law office left me little time to take more than one-week family excursions into the woods and lakes of northern Michigan and an occasional weekend for professional meetings in cities such as Boston and San Francisco. Barbara's experience was similar, although she had done some traveling in Europe, the Middle East, and South America.

By the time we met, our children had left the nest. We began to travel together, going on several Sierra Club backpacking trips that lasted seven to ten days. Our international trips were initially limited to the tourist magnets of Europe. But after encountering one too many tourist buses, we resolved to seek more isolated, less popular destinations.

In 2002, we went to Vietnam for three weeks, hiring occasional drivers and guides. We had protested against the Vietnam War, and I had counseled and represented draft resisters in my law practice. Not many Americans had explored the country since the war ended. We were curious as to the reactions the Vietnamese would have to us. Rather than displaying hostility, or worse, because of our government's destruction of their country, the Vietnamese, friendly and businesslike, were concerned only with what we wanted to buy. "The war?" they said. "Which war? The Japanese? The French? The Chinese? The Cambodians? Oh, the Americans! Oh, that's all over. Let me show you our new line of silk shirts."

We were hooked. Thus began our odyssey, usually to countries that caused friends and family to worry (needlessly) about our safety and judgment. Over the years, they have learned to accept our choices and simply to ask where we are going next. Their curiosity about our experiences gave rise to the idea for this book.

In recent years, we have incorporated trekking into our travel plans. Hiking from village to village and staying in villages at night has given us the opportunity to see how people in other societies live. This is a felicitous way to learn about other cultures—to eat with people, stay in their homes, go into their fields, watch their dances, listen to their music, and hear their stories, myths, and legends. People are proud of their culture and delighted that friendly strangers are interested. The accommodations are certainly not luxurious—most lack indoor plumbing—but the rewards are immense. Leaving our comfort zone has expanded our view of the world.

We trekked and stayed with Sherpas in the Langtang Valley of Nepal; tribal village farmers in the Shan hill country of Myanmar; rubber tree farmers in China's Yunnan province; the cliff-dwelling Dogon along Mali's Bandiagara Escarpment; tribes in the mountains, rivers, and coastal range of Papua New Guinea; and the Baka Pygmy of the Dja Forest Reserve in Cameroon.

We have developed a particular interest in indigenous peoples whose cultures have survived relatively intact for centuries–their art, music, dance, sexual mores, economic and political hierarchy, and spirituality. How have they resisted change under the pressures of economic globalization and the incursions of western culture?

Why do they resist? Are they happy? If so, what do they know that we don't?

Travel is also a way of gaining information about political issues and events of importance. Face-to-face communication with people directly involved in these situations provides valuable insight not available in our mass media.

Other than in unique circumstances, such as in Gaza in 2009 and Cuba in 2013, we avoid tours and choose to travel with only a guide and driver. Because of this, people in both isolated and populous areas often approach us with a smile to ask where we are from and why we have come to their country. In China, they even asked how much money I earned. They frequently invite us into their homes and offer coffee or tea, something that rarely happens when a tour bus pulls up and twenty tourists emerge.

We are not young—I was born in 1938, and Barbara, in 1944. However, we work out a lot and are in good shape, despite our share of late-life malfunctions. I have early Parkinsonism and recently had open-heart surgery, while Barbara has just recovered from knee-replacement surgery. But to the extent that we can travel and trek, we will continue to do so. Our hope is to inspire others who are ambulatory, curious, adventurous, and thoughtful to do the same. This is perhaps the last generation to have the opportunity to observe these cultures before their ways of life or their environments succumb to globalization. And, unfortunately, because of subsequent events, we may already have been among the last tourists to visit some of the amazing places in this world—Syria, Mali, eastern Turkey, Venezuela, and perhaps even Egypt.

In most of the nonwestern cultures we visited, older people, both men and women, are treated with great respect and treasured for their wisdom. Members of the community ensure that their elders are fed and protected from harm. This includes visitors, and our gray hairs made us frequent beneficiaries of this tradition. In Papua New

Guinea, we were made honorary elders in a Highland village. In Bali, our young guide asked me how I felt about life, at my age. I thought before I answered and said, "It's been a full life—and getting fuller."

Traveling while older has had its amusing moments as well. While going up the trail in Nepal, we encountered a young man coming down who looked at our gray hair and told us that the only trekking his father did was from the living room couch to the refrigerator. In Palmyra, Syria, a young woman told us that she thought it was "wonderful that elderly couples are traveling together." In Venezuela, a checkpoint guard looked at our passports and asked our guide, "Where are their children? Why are their children not taking care of them?" And so on. But most often, people are amazed that we are strong enough to visit their remote areas and admire us for doing so.

This volume includes only some of the trips we have taken. It is based on our memories, my journals, and Barbara's photos.

Perhaps the other trips—to eastern Turkey, Lebanon, Syria, Tunisia, Laos, and Cambodia among them—will form the core of another volume. We hope to add to that list in the future.

Dennis James, 2016

Papua New Guinea:

EXPECT THE UNEXPECTED

It is late afternoon in the rain forest of Papua New Guinea, in the coastal area called Tufi. Barbara and I have been trekking for seven hours on steep, slippery terrain along a barely discernable trail from the village of Tumari, where we had spent the night, to Koruwe Bay.

The trail passes through rain forest, whose one-hundred-foot-high canopy houses birds of paradise, the fashionistas of avian society, sporting yard-long tail feathers, spiral antennae, and plumage like the Medici court. The trail skirts carefully tended village flower gardens of bougainvillea, hibiscus, and frangipani and wanders through patches of wild orchids and groves of giant tree ferns, like those in paintings by Henri Rousseau.

We climb and descend hillsides of chest-high kunai grass whose sharp edges cut exposed flesh. Grab a wad of it and you'll come away with bloody fingers. So, despite the heat, Barbara and I wear long pants and long sleeves. Our principal guide, Clarence, and three of his fellow villagers (two cousins, Donald and Eddie, and Phillip, a village elder) are barefoot and wear shorts and T-shirts. Their skin, especially the soles of their feet, is toughened by a lifetime spent shoeless on this harsh terrain. Their toes are splayed and widely separated. Their feet grip surfaces that our boots skid and slide on.

It is hot and humid. Tolerably so under the forest canopy, which filters out some of the rays, but on high burner in the treeless fields of kunai. We have stopped only briefly to eat bananas and papaya and to drink water. Now we can see the sea in the distance—the Solomon Sea, part of the South Pacific Ocean—a shining wedge of turquoise framed by the black branches of a mahogany tree. There must only be a few hundred yards to go. We pick up the pace.

"We are almost there," Clarence says. "Only one more hard part."

The trees thin out and we can see more of the bay's inlet. Suddenly, we come to the edge of a lava rock cliff, with a sheer drop of sixty feet between us and the last stretch of the trail. I point toward the bottom of the cliff and look at Clarence, who smiles and nods.

"Last hard part," he says. "We will help."

I look down and can feel my acrophobia morphing into vertigo. "Let's go," says Clarence. "You'll make it down."

"Yes," I say. "The question is how."

With Clarence on my left and his cousin Donald on my right, we creep downward, facing the lava wall, on what I can now see is a six- to eight-inch ledge, half covered with shrubbery, that snakes across the cliff face in descending switchbacks.

"Put foot here," Clarence says. "Foot there." Twenty minutes go by and we are halfway down. I take my eyes off the trail to see Barbara above with Phillip and Eddie hovering over her. Above them, smiling and waiting patiently at the top of the cliff are Clarence's wife and two daughters. We come to a particularly difficult segment of the trail that is blocked by a large shrub poking through the black rock. As Clarence and Donald confer on how we are going to negotiate this obstacle I drift into rueful reflection on our situation.

It is June 2014. I am seventy-six. Barbara is seventy. What are we doing here? I'm exhausted, covered with sweat and mud, clinging to a cliff face. We should be sipping Pernod at Les Deux Magots café on the Boulevard Saint-Germain or wandering through the back streets of the Trastevere in Rome. Why did we go trekking in Papua New Guinea instead?

Why Papua New Guinea?

On one of our visits to the Metropolitan Museum of Art in New York City, we wander into a gallery of Oceanic Art and are quickly struck by the sophistication and intricacy of the wood carvings from Papua New Guinea.

"Papua New Guinea," Barbara says. "That would be an interesting place to visit."

Papua New Guinea, often referred to as PNG by its citizens, is the poster child for a destination that is enticingly exotic but too difficult to get to and get around in. Nevertheless, with the help of our travel agent, we put together a unique itinerary that involves three- to four-day treks in three zones of Papua New Guinea—the Highlands, the Sepik River, and the Tufi Coast, interspersed with one-day stays at Western-style hotels. On the treks, we will be encountering and staying with New Guineans who live almost entirely on what they grow or find in the bush, who value pigs more than money, and who rarely encounter white people. The agent assures us that the New Guineans are very friendly and hospitable.

We spend a couple of weeks gradually talking ourselves into a New Guinea trek, trying to rationalize the discomfort and expense of the long transit necessary to get there and discount warnings about the perils in-country. Our friends are no help in allaying our concerns. A few of their comments include:

"Papua New Guinea!? Are you crazy?"

"They have malaria and dengue fever."

"They eat people there. They ate Michael Rockefeller."

"What's the matter with Hawaii?"

But the most frequent question is "Why Papua New Guinea?" I get tired of answering, perhaps because I am not sure, myself. But PNG's paleontological history indicates that many tribes today live substantially as they have since the end of the most recent ice age. These tribal cultures may soon be marginalized by the relentless intrusion of global capital seeking new sources of timber, minerals, and hydrocarbons, and new locations for luxury tourist development. This may be a last chance to meet and learn from people who are living almost as humans had lived twelve thousand years ago. We do some peak scrambling in the White Mountains of New Hampshire just to be sure our legs are ready.

Finally, we pay the fare and mark our calendars for June 6, 2014, to June 29, 2014. Our travel agent, who has traveled in New Guinea before, notes that a popular saying there is, "Expect the unexpected." Then he laughs.

Getting There

We spend thirty cramped hours in stuffy aluminum tubes, plus six or seven hours of layovers in sterile, sprawling airports—New York to Los Angeles to Brisbane, Australia, to Port Moresby, Papua New Guinea. The fifteen-hour flight from LA to Brisbane is in almost total darkness as the plane races ahead of the sunrise. We fly through several time zones and cross the international dateline, eventually losing contact with any prior circadian rhythm. Dinners are served when our bodies expect sleep. Snacks appear when we hope for meals. Fitful slumber is interrupted by flight attendants hawking duty-free booze.

Barbara and I do the *New York Times* crossword puzzles together. We read. But, strapped in my seat and constantly snacking with little sleep and no exercise, I feel like a bloated zombie by the time the plane lands in Port Moresby on the southern coast of PNG.

We retrieve our carry-on luggage and backpacks and stagger through Customs and Immigration, then make our way to the ground transportation deck. The heat and humidity of the night tells us something about what the coming days will be like.

I see a van from the Gateway Hotel and flag it down. The lobby of the Gateway is crowded with foreign and New Guinean businessmen. The hotel staff is crisp and efficient. But when I claim our reservations, a desk clerk informs me, crisply and efficiently, that I have none. To make matters worse, our local guide, who was to meet us at the hotel with the requisite paperwork, does not show. Fortunately, we are able to reach our local contact, Emanuel, a calm and mild-mannered young man, who, as he did so often during our trip, fixes everything with a couple of phone calls.

Port Moresby (population of 255,000) is the capital and largest city. It is not the Paris of the South Pacific. Much of it is squalid, dirty, and dangerous. Gangs of unemployed young men hang out on the corners. Tourists are advised not to walk alone or too far from the hotel at night. Jet lagged, we eat at the hotel and go to bed.

The next morning, Emanuel comes by to introduce himself and advise us that our scheduled flight from Port Moresby to the coastal city of Madang has been canceled because the aircraft was "inoperative." He says this without any indication of surprise, disbelief, or frustration. Instead, we will fly to the city of Mount Hagen in the Highlands. Thus begins our experience with "expect the unexpected."

Our flight to Mount Hagen (population of 45,000) is uneventful. We check in at the Highlander Hotel. The city, which has a Nursing College and a Bible College, is otherwise a smaller version of Port Moresby. The next morning, we meet our local guide, Steve, who takes us on a short tour of some of the farms on the periphery of the city. The farms are incredibly neat, with fields of taro root, cabbage, sweet potato, and pumpkin, as well as small orchards of papaya and mango. The fields, each about a rectangular half acre, are bordered by worn dirt paths and hedges with orange flowers. One of the rectangles contains nothing but orchids—not for sale, just for the family's décor.

Because of their proximity to a large town, these farmers enjoy urban amenities such as electricity, running water, autos, modern building materials, etc. I suspect this will not be the case in the Highland bush, beyond the reach of New Guinea's few roads.

PNG 101

The vast majority of Highlanders had no contact with the outside world until the 1930s, when two gold-prospecting Australian brothers, seeking locations for exploration, flew over central New Guinea. The Australians assumed, as did all Europeans, that the interior was an uninhabited, mountainous rain forest. They were astonished to find a million people living off of neatly laid-out gardens on the mountain slopes and high valleys. These New Guineans were equally astonished to find that there was a world of human beings outside their small villages. In fact, the early inhabitants typically did not even know the people in villages beyond their immediate neighbors. Eight hundred and thirty-one distinct languages are spoken in Papua New Guinea, one-twelfth of all languages spoken worldwide. Everyone made up their own language because talking with other villagers was not a priority.

In the early nineteenth century, the arrival of foreign sailors promoted the development and use of a pidgin form of English called *Tok Pisin*, also simply referred to as *Pidgin*, which ultimately spread to the interior. Although English is now the official language of the government, Tok Pisin remains the language of the people, who continue to use their own tribal tongues as well. Although Tok Pisin is clearly derived from English, we were unable to understand a word.

People of Papuan and Melanesian ancestry have occupied the Highlands for thirty thousand years. They entered New Guinea from Indonesia and Southeast Asia during the last great Ice Age, at which time there was a land bridge linking Asia, New Guinea, and Australia. By 10,000 BC, the seas had risen, isolating New Guinea from Indonesia and Asia.

The Highlanders found that between the altitudes of four to nine thousand feet, they could grow almost anything on the lava-infused soil. And there was plenty of fresh water. Above nine thousand feet, it was too cold for crops and below four thousand, it was too wet and infested with malarial swamps. What developed were self-contained, self-sustaining islands of humanity with no particular interest in any contact with their neighbors, except for the occasional raiding party seeking wives or avenging some trespass or injury perpetrated by the other.

As for modern transportation in the Highland interior, there are probably more miles of aircraft landing strips than miles of roads. There are 562 airstrip locations indicated on the International Travel Map alone and just a few sad ribbons of highway, mostly along the coast. There are no railroads. Flying over the interior, we realize that the main reason for this disparity is geography. One-third of New Guinea consists of steep mountain ranges covered with rain forest. From the air, it looks like a rumpled green blanket with lighter green patches of crops and kunai grass. Building roads in this terrain, even when technically possible, is prohibitively expensive. To get from anywhere in the interior to any place else in PNG you fly, walk, or float. Most Highlanders have limited options. Even if there is a nearby airstrip, flying is costly, and not everyone can afford it. If they are not on a navigable stretch of one of New Guinea's great river systems, they cannot paddle. And, given the topography, even the fittest can't walk very far. So they remain out of contact, subsisting, but not flourishing—essentially living as their ancestors had.

For those who can afford it, a few small airlines, some run by missionaries, provide internal transport. These planes function like the local buses in New York City, sometimes landing and taking off three or four times during a two-hundred-mile trip. The planes are frequently taken out of service for repair. Spare parts are available only in a few larger city airports. Most airstrips have no terminal, control tower, runway lights, or repair facilities. With luck, there is a small metal-roofed shack or cement block structure to shelter waiting passengers.

The roads that do exist are compromised by monstrous potholes. This is true on the highway as well as in the center of the larger towns like Port Moresby, Mount Hagen, and Wewak.

Simbai and Waim

In the early morning, we check out of the hotel in Mount Hagen to get to the airstrip at six a.m. for our flight to Simbai, a typically small, isolated village on the slope of the Bismarck Range. One of its elders, Dickson Kangi, maintains a group of guesthouses.

The gate to our airline, Mission Air, is closed and locked. No one is around. We dump our backpacks on the ground by the cyclone fence, sit, and wait. A kindly security guard opens the gate for us so we can get to a bench with a shed roof over it for shade. A few other passengers show up and stand around; most are men in work clothes being flown to a job someplace. We, a curiosity to the locals, introduce ourselves, and everyone is very friendly. Nothing happens until eight a.m., when the pilot and ticket-taker arrive. Checking everyone through and weighing everything, including the passengers, takes an excruciating hour. After we pile into a twenty-seat, single-engine plane, we fly below the peaks, witnessing a wide-angle view of an intensely verdant, roadless landscape, dotted with villages and squared-off gardens on the slopes.

We land near a village and take off again ten minutes later. More mountain greenery scrolls by our window, and then the plane banks

Sunrise, Waim Village

for a landing on a single runway airstrip in a high valley. It rolls to a turnaround, taxis to a parking zone, and shuts down. There is no tower, no terminal. About one hundred people are standing or sitting on an embankment overlooking the runway. Dickson and his assistant, Ronald, walk up to greet us, then the crowd follows as we are led up a broad, winding path leading to the village. Many come up to shake our hands and introduce themselves, smiling and laughing. The men and boys wear well-used western-style shorts and shirts, as do the women, although some wear skirts. Most speak English to us and Tok Pisin to each other, but soon we hear chanting in an entirely different language.

As we turn a bend in the pathway, ten men and a little boy in full tribal regalia approach. They wear only leafy loincloths. Their faces and bodies are painted in stripes and dots of bright yellow, red, white, and black. They have rattles on their ankles and multiple strands of cowrie shells around their necks. Tall crowns that look like the shakos of the Coldstream Guards, made of the black feathers of birds of paradise, adorn their heads. Their noses' septums are pierced with boars' tusks or abalone shells. Four men keep time for the intricate shuffling, hip-twitching dance and the repeated chanted verses of the song with hour-glass shaped, yard-long kundu drums. Others carry traditional weapons, slender seven-foot-long spears and axes, bows, and arrows. These are strapping fellows, tall and muscled, with heavy scarification on their backs and chests and complex tattoos on their faces.

One of the dancers chooses the song, leads off, and the rest join in. The little boy, wearing a similar outfit, mimics the movements of his elders in the middle of the formation. This dance and song is one of welcome, incorporating us into the village as honorary elders. We are grateful and impressed that we have witnessed an ancient ritual.

Dancing and chanting, the group leads us to the village square, where they finish their sing-sing and store their headdresses and traditional artifacts in a hut. They allow us to look in the doorway. In the dim light of the windowless hut, we see masks, icons, head-dresses, and weapons hung on the walls, like the wardrobe of a tropical Valhalla.

All of the men of the village have holes in their septum. It is a traditional rite of passage to adulthood, Dickson explains. The holes remain unadorned unless the men participate in a dance or another special occasion.

Dickson shows us his guesthouse compound, which is thoughtfully laid out with four small cabins in a row facing a central grassy square and a large cabin at a right angle to the others. On the other side of the square is a tall, round meetinghouse where meals are fixed and served and where there is a warming room with a fireplace. A thatched hut serves as a latrine and another as a bathhouse with sun-heated water. Our cabin is of ample size with two platforms for beds and sleeping pads, and a front porch equipped with chairs and a stool.

The grounds are like a botanical garden, with variegated flowers, ferns, and plants. The grass is cut, and stones line the borders of the flower gardens and the paths. Neatly cut drainage ditches keep the area reasonably dry during the rainy season. All structures are on three- to four-foot-high stilts that accommodate heavy ground runoff. There is not a speck of litter on the grounds. During a short tour of the village, I note that the same orderliness and harmony with the surrounding natural beauty characterizes all of the homes, gardens, and pathways in Simbai. A bearded old man in a loin cloth, well past his days of heavy lifting, tends the village's orchid garden. Is this public beautification unique to Simbai, a lucky village with an airstrip and a trekker's jumping-off point?

As we tour the grounds, we encounter an elderly expatriate, J. M., who has heard that two tourists from the States are visiting. He invites himself to dinner with us at Dickson's and strolls off. Dickson is not pleased.

Dinner is a spread of taro root, sweet potato, white potato, greens, fried bananas, and papaya (called *paw-paw*). It is a typical Highland dinner, and everything comes fresh from Dickson's family's garden. The only add-ons are two cans of tuna, obtained, no doubt, with some difficulty.

We soon learn why Dickson is irritated by J. M.'s intrusion: J. M. monopolizes the conversation for hours, talking mostly about himself. He talks about his position as an Associate Professor of Anthropology at Divine Word University and about the time he was in the PNG government as First Secretary to the Prime Minister and, later, the Minister of Public Works. After J. M. leaves, Dickson expresses his disappointment at not being able to spend the dinner talking with us. Apparently, J. M. had married a local woman who had died three years ago. "J. M. can't get over it," he explains. "He is very lonely." We look up Divine Word University after we return home and find that it does, in fact, exist. It is a Catholic university that receives government support, and J. M. is listed as faculty.

According to Dickson, it is rare for anyone in the village to go hungry. If a person is injured or a family is unable to grow or tend their garden, the whole village sees to it that they are fed. The gardens are very productive and there is always enough for all. However, the villagers have no source of income with which to buy medicine, clothes, tools, generators, or trips to the cities by plane. Some time ago, when the world market for vanilla surged, the government urged everyone to grow vanilla. So, the New Guineans did, as did many others around the world, causing the market to collapse. Dickson's hope is that the government will help develop tourism. I tell him, "If people in Europe and the States learn about the beauty and hospitality of your country, they will come—particularly the younger people."

He replies, "And adventuresome, older people as well."

The next day, we are to trek to Waim, about five hours away, stay a day and two nights, then trek back to Simbai. There is no airstrip in Waim. How will it compare to Simbai?

The trail to Waim is up and down steep slopes with loose rocks, a baked coagulate of rotted plants and red clay the viscosity of heavy grease. It is hot and wet. Every step is a potential sliding fall into the muck. Dickson says the guidebook rates the trail as "moderate," though he has told them it should be "difficult." I agree.

When we finally arrive at Waim, an all-female sing-sing group in traditional dress greets us. They do not wear the feathered crowns worn by the men but have orchids in their hair, a symbol, we are told, of happiness. The village green is on a broad, flat ledge of several acres perched above a deep valley formed by the intersection of two mountain ranges. A soccer field is laid out, and a primary school is located in one corner of the green. Flowers are everywhere, in ordered composition in the village gardens and in chaotic profusion on the jungle trails.

Our guesthouse is similar to the one in Simbai. We dump our overnight packs and wander the village, introducing ourselves. Everyone takes our hand and smiles, their red lips evincing the prevalence of betel nut consumption, particularly among the elderly. This ubiquitous chewing habit, with its mild narcotic effect, eventually destroys the gums and teeth. The betel nut is chewed with a lime concoction that generates a bright-red coloring of saliva, gums, tongue, lips, and teeth, leading to friendly, scarlet, single-toothed smiles. The New Guineans call it PNG lipstick, their national drug, a social concoction similar to Western wine. Parents even introduce it to their children.

The night is surprisingly chilly, bringing on a polyrhythmic insect and bird chorus of symphonic proportions.

In the morning, the sun ignites the surrounding mountain tops, and a sea of fog fills the valley below. We decide to visit the school, which is a two-room affair with rough benches for the students. The teacher accepts our gift of two dozen ballpoint pens and a world map. Later, he takes the children out for assembly on the field, where forty or so youngsters line up in rows, singing the national anthem and a song welcoming us. Some adults who are studying English at the school are also in line. The teacher tells the assembly about our little gifts, and there is a burst of applause. He asks me to make a few comments, and I tell them how welcome we feel and how beautiful their village and country are. Then the teacher asks everyone in the assembly to shake our hands and introduce themselves by name in English, which they happily proceed to do, in orderly lines. We are moved by the genuine pleasure they express.

As the fog burns off, Ronald takes us on a tour of the village, pointing out new and old structures and thriving crops: potatoes, cabbage, taro root, greens, pumpkin. He invites us to observe an extended family prepare a cooking pit feast in honor of a family event. The women construct a woodpile filled with large rocks. A man crouching on the ground spins a pointed stick against a piece of dry bark until the bark begins to smoke. He blows on the smoking bark until it glows, ignites a handful of fine thatch, and carries the burning thatch to the woodpile to start the fire, taking all of five minutes. I can hardly believe it. The Highlanders have no matches, and they start fires the same way they have for untold centuries.

The women dig shallow pits and, when the stones are hot, fill the pits with alternating layers of hot stones, banana leaves, slow cooking vegetables, more stones, more banana leaves, and faster-cooking vegetables until the pit is full. They cover the pit with banana leaves, socialize for an hour, remove the cover, and eat their way down to the bottom of the pit. I sample the greens. They are pungent and hot, like mustard greens.

As in Simbai, the locals practice the same attention to orderliness and appreciation of the natural beauty around them—decorative stones and flower gardens lining the village paths, even the one to the latrine; a mini-hut with a thatched roof; crab grass on the green cut short.

The trek back to Simbai seems more difficult. We fall occasionally and are covered with mud by the time we reach Simbai. Fortunately, we hike the distance in two hours less than we did going the other way. Over our objections, Dickson enlists some women in the village to wash out our hiking clothes.

Over a lovely dinner around a fire, Ronald describes the quandary facing young people in the Highlands. They remain where they are, in a subsistence economy, with little chance of getting the education needed to obtain employment elsewhere, other than temporary, menial labor jobs for low wages. Remaining in their villages in the Highlands assures them of a physical, psychological, and spiritual support system within their clan's traditions that is lifelong and steadfast. And the only way to successfully break out of this subsistence society and join the consumer economy of the cities of the world is to leave the village for education or training in the cities, where they are alone, bereft of family and clan support, and subject to the temptations of gang life. Many have succumbed to these urban pressures. What is needed, Ronald says, is some income flow to the Highlands that doesn't require the exile of its youth.

Silent, we watch the fire in the darkening room.

We think about several possible approaches: develop tourism or even means of transportation to bring the tribes' abundant goods and resources to market. But weak infrastructure and government neglect make these solutions unlikely.

Ronald has raised a dilemma we have confronted on several trips: the conflict between development and preservation of a unique indigenous culture. Development can come in many forms, some more harmful than others. Our worry is that development and preservation cannot coexist and that development always wins.

We have also seen on our travels villages populated only by older people and cities filled with the young whose dreams have not materialized.

To us, these indigenous cultures are complex, with beautiful music and art and people who cooperate rather than compete with one another. We think they should be preserved. However, we worry that even relatively benign intrusions such as ecotourism, which would provide jobs and other services, would also degrade these ways of life. So how can we, creatures of the West, say that others should not be able to try to secure the comforts and advances we take for granted?

We tell Ronald that we will encourage our friends to visit the Highlands, but the truth is that we have no adequate response for him. Only smoldering embers remain in the sand pit. Ronald stands and offers to escort us to our cabin.

The next trek is from Simbai to Kundum Hostel. It is a good trail, six hours of up and down but decent footing. There is long sun exposure and we take all precautions—lots of water, frequent stops, sun block, electrolytes, and, occasionally, an umbrella. Ronald has brought

Ronald and family

along his wife, an excellent cook with a lovely smile, and his young daughter, who is eager to practice her English with us.

Kundum Hostel is described as a birder's delight. Unfortunately, the birds are nowhere to be seen. But the setting is beautiful, and we are warmly greeted by the elders with their toothless red smiles and fresh, tasty food. We fall asleep to the raucous cries of the unseen birds, a lullaby compared to the sirens, car horns, and loud music we hear at night back home in Brooklyn.

In the morning, we retrace our steps on the sizzling path to Simbai for five and a half hours. As we approach Simbai, we pass the home of the head of the American Southern Baptist Missionary Project. It is a large modern dwelling that would not be out of place in the wealthy suburbs of any American metropolis. It is surrounded by an off-putting high cyclone fence. Dickson says the clerical occupant is there only a few months a year.

We spend a pleasant last night in Simbai after a good dinner, sitting around the warming fire. The next morning, Dickson says our flight to Mount Hagen has been "canceled." It was to be the first leg of our transfer to Wewak on the way to the Sepik River. The travel agency has chartered a special flight for us, which will also be transporting some "foodstuffs" to cut the cost of the charter. Sure enough, a small silver plane appears over the valley, banks, lands, rolls up to the turnaround, and parks. Local men rush up to the cargo door and begin tossing boxes of noodles onto the tarmac. Another stream of men files down the hill from the village with fifty-kilogram sacks of coffee beans on their backs, which they deposit in the plane. Waved into the plane's cabin, we find we are the only passengers. We sit on the floor behind a lashed-down pile of coffee bean sacks that fills the rest of the plane. There are no flight attendants, no instructions, and no lunch, but there is plenty of leg room.

Two plane changes, five landings and take-offs, and ten packages of complimentary biscuits later, we land in Wewak, a coastal town, for an overnight stay at the Boutique Hotel. We enjoy a swim in the pool, a hot shower, a spicy seafood stew, and a night on a good mattress.

Sepik River

The next day we are driven by Land Rover to Pawgi, a town on the Middle Sepik River, picking up our guide, James Korgo, on the way. We dump our gear into a thirty-foot motorized dugout canoe and travel downstream for an hour to Korogo, a village spread along the left bank of the Sepik.

The Sepik, milk chocolate in color, with endless bends and curls, is one of the longest rivers in Papua New Guinea. It is more than a mile wide in its lower reaches. A distinct riverain culture affiliated with the Crocodile Clan has stimulated an extraordinarily rich production of wood carvings in the Middle Sepik villages—mostly masks and statues depicting spirits and ancestors. There is more tourist traffic, commerce, and exposure to Eurasian culture here than in the Highlands.

James Korgo is, as the Godfather would say, "a serious man." His family compound on the river encompasses several acres and a lake. There is a central house, on six-foot stilts to accommodate the Sepik's annual flooding, with four rooms and a kitchen area. Under construction is a guesthouse and houses for his sons and daughters. He is confident that the guesthouse will be occupied regularly. He does his own carpentry, just as he carves his own dugout canoes. He is the local magistrate, charged with keeping the peace in his district.

We tour the village with James, walking along the bank, greeting the residents. We come to the remnants of a spirit house or *haus tambarans* a group of carved and weathered pillars bereft of roof or walls. The carved images reflect the Crocodile Clan's creation myth, which involves a crocodile that mates with a female human, who gives birth to two eagles.

The village's new spirit house is a large two-story structure with hardwood pillars and a steep thatched roof that swoops up in front like the prow of a sailing ship. The roof is topped with the mother

Spirit house, Sepik River

figure giving birth. We enter the spirit house and find several men, two in tribal dress. The two beat out a rhythmic welcome on bath-tub-sized hollow logs. While we walk around the grounds, James engages the men in discussion of some complaint they have, speaking in Tok Pisin. He hears them out, speaks patiently but assertively, and resolves the matter.

A spare room in James's main house is used for guests pending completion of the guesthouse. It is separated from the master bedroom and the other rooms by woven grass walls, the arrangement not conducive to privacy. Dinner consists of everyone sitting on the floor of a common room with dishes passed around—vegetables supplemented by bony but tasty river fish.

I sleep well except for a necessary trip to the family toilet, which involves descending and later ascending a shaky bamboo ladder and walking one hundred feet to the latrine. This is more or less the situation in all of the guesthouses we occupy. Doing this jaunt, half-awake and with a dim flashlight, can lead to spatial disorientation resulting in a nasty fall or getting lost in terra incognita.

Over the next couple of days, we travel in James's motorized canoe down the river to villages noted for their wood carvings. These are the type of artifacts we saw in the Metropolitan Museum of Art and which piqued our interest in PNG. We stop for provisions along the way and end up buying a bride price, a carving that men traditionally give their future in-laws before the wedding. The piece is carved in the shape of a stylized crocodile with rare circular shells attached to its back. This type of shell was at one time used as currency. The seller tells us that this was his mother's bride price. Putting aside the pre-feminist nature of the work, we think it is beautiful.

One village, Palumbei, is particularly interesting. Located a few hundred yards from the river, it looks like a Hollywood set for the musical *South Pacific*. Coconut palms tower over a manicured village green the size of a soccer field. Graceful thatched huts on stilts are spaced dozens of yards apart. Several narrow lagoons, full of water lilies and crossed by footbridges, traverse the area outside the green where the rest of the village people live. Two spirit houses, each belonging to a separate clan, stand at each end of the green. At the center of the green are the remains of an older spirit house, destroyed during the Japanese occupation in World War II.

Several men lounge in one of the spirit houses, sitting around and talking. Although these structures are used during initiation rites and other ceremonies, on a day-to-day basis they function as a place for men (not women) to hang out. Graciously, an exception is made for Barbara.

We are greeted by a traditional sing-sing. In contrast to what we observed in the Highlands, men and women dance and sing together. The men emerge from a spirit house, forming a circle. The women come out from a grove of trees, forming an outer circle, their skirts swirling. All wear elaborate face paint.

There is a small Christian chapel on the green as well, its wooden walls painted white with a metal roof and a cross on top. Purportedly, New Guinea is now mostly Christian, although it is obvious that the vast majority also adhere to their traditional animism. I want to know whether the Christian clergy discourages practice of these ancient rituals, so I ask James what faith he professes or follows, if any. To my surprise, he looses a tirade against organized religion of any sort. James is Christian, but he has no use for the churches that are "corrupt, hypocritical, and full of jealousy and inner power struggles." James prays directly to his creator without an intermediary. He tells me that the Catholic Church is more accepting of traditional practices than are the Protestant churches. He acknowledges one significant achievement of the Christian ascendancy: "It kept us from killing one another."

Traveling on the huge river is mesmerizing. It loops and almost doubles back on itself. Aside from the hum of the motor, there is the stillness common to big rivers. Snow-white egrets and cranes beat up out of the shallows, flying to their nests in the high trees and gorging on river fish and frogs that they will regurgitate for their young. Early morning fog envelops the river, limiting visibility to thirty feet. James, in the stern, can hardly see the bow of the canoe, let alone the riverbanks. Yet he powers up and steers on instinct, having lived on and traversed the river all his life. The fog burns off, but hours later a sudden accumulation of dark clouds appears downstream, and James makes for the left bank. We pull up to the dock of a small village, jump out of the canoe, and reach a thatched shelter just before the downpour hits. The rain lasts thirty minutes. It wanes and we thank our surprised hosts, hop back in, bail out the rainwater, and push off.

We spend a rare uncomfortable night in a village on a tributary of the Sepik. It was advised of our imminent arrival, was presumably paid the guesthouse rental fee, but is totally unprepared for us. The room is tiny and hot, with no floor pads, blankets, or pillows. These items are offered for an additional overpriced purchase. Fortunately, we are carrying inflatable camping pads and pillows, which we use to keep us up off the rough bamboo floor.

The village is the only one of all those we stay at or pass through that looks run down. Paths are indistinct, and drainage ditches are crossed by single shaky logs, rather than by several solid boards or sturdy bamboo poles lashed together, as in other villages. Holed-out hulls of large dugout canoes lie rotting on the ground. James decries the waste and says he may make an offer to buy one and fix it. Children with distended bellies run naked after us, asking for candy. Further from the river is a hut where an old man sells carved artifacts. They are mostly simplistic versions of more complicated and subtle works we have seen elsewhere. He brings out a green stone the size of a ciabatta roll, etched with unknown script. He says it was found in a cave with bones and skulls hundreds of years old. We are interested, but James takes us aside and says the inscriptions have been recently made by machine, not hand. We pass on it. There seems to be a pervasive demoralization in this place, for reasons unknown to us.

Our last day on the river takes us to Angoram, near the mouth of the Sepik where we are to be picked up and driven back to Wewak for the night. The following day, we are to fly to Port Moresby to connect with a flight to the Tufi Coast for the last leg of our three-part trekking tour. We climb into a big Toyota Land Rover 4x4 with the driver, Leo. James hitches a ride into town with us, sitting in the truck's bed with three of Leo's young sons. The highway is, as expected, a nightmare of giant potholes and washouts, which Leo avoids for the most part. The ones he hits bounce the truck like a basketball. Suddenly, the truck veers off the road on its own volition. Leo manages to wrestle it back on the asphalt and brings it to a halt. After he spends a few minutes on the ground under the left suspension, Leo announces that we have lost a nut needed for the steering mechanism. I am dubious about our chances of reaching Wewak before dark. Leo's boys go back to where the truck went wild and look for the nut in the road, returning within five minutes, smiling broadly. They have found it. We are in for one more stroke of luck—Leo is able to borrow a wrench from a friend who happens to be passing by in his car. Within a half hour, we are back in business.

We spend the night in Wewak at the Boutique Hotel, where a number of businessmen are also staying. In the morning, while we wait in the lobby for our ride to the airport, I notice a lone westerner sitting on a couch, doodling with his iPhone, looking somewhat morose. I ask where he's from. "Spain," he says. I ask what brings him to Wewak, Papua New Guinea. "Tuna," he replies, like someone else might say "ball bearings," or "plastics." Further inquiry discloses that he is a scout for a big fish processing company and is interested in the tuna runs in the Solomon Sea. His company is considering the possibility of seine net fishing off the coast using New Guineans for cheap labor. He discloses this hesitantly, almost apologetically. He is a sad, little man who, I believe, senses the adverse social consequences for New Guineans of what he does.

We fly back to Port Moresby and are ready the next day for a two-stop short flight to the Tufi Coast. Once again, the unexpected intervenes.

Tufi . . . or Not Tufi

There is no problem with the first stop of our plane on its way to Tufi from Port Moresby. We land and take off within ten minutes. The second stop is at a town called Popondetta, twenty minutes from Tufi by air.

Some passengers deplane. Barbara and I and the other Tufi-bound passengers wait in the plane on the runway, eating airline biscuits. Unexpectedly, the flight attendant asks us to leave and wait in the terminal, a two-room cinder block structure. We sit on some benches facing the runway and watch the pilot, copilot, and terminal

War detritus, Popondetta Airport

manager confer on the tarmac. The flight attendant emerges from the plane carrying a case of bottled water and distributes the water to the waiting passengers.

Finally, the copilot says that in his walk around the plane during this layover he saw some hydraulic fluid running down a seam in the fuselage. He offers to show it to me. Sure enough, there it is, a translucent ooze an inch wide, running down the side of the plane. The leak could cause hydraulic pressure to drop, and the pilot could lose control of the wing flaps and would have a tough time landing.

We wait for an engineer to arrive, talking with the pilots and smiling at the other passengers, who do not speak standard English. The pilot is from Australia and the copilot from India. They are young, in their thirties. They work a staggered schedule of two months on and three weeks off. They miss home. The pilot says, however, that he has learned more about flying in one year in PNG than he did in ten years in Australia.

There is no viable alternate route, by land or sea, to Tufi. We wander out to the road where a market of rude tables and canopies has sprung up just outside the airport gate, doing a brisk business in betel nuts and fatty sausages. Barbara finds the women's washroom locked and goes over to the plane with the pilot who turns on the engines so the plane's toilet will flush. "It's the least I can do," he says. I wander the airport grounds and find the wreckage of an American B-24 Liberator bomber from World War II, one of many that litter the island. During the war, these planes were made in Detroit, where I was born and raised.

Relatives of the passengers from Popondetta who were waiting for the plane arrive with steaming platters of chicken stew. The recipients graciously offer to share the food with us, noting that we have been nibbling on airline biscuits all day. I gratefully accept. We thank the family (grandmother, mother, and granddaughter) with a dozen ballpoint pens, and they are thrilled, especially the granddaughter.

Later, I fall asleep on one of the benches in the building. When I awake, the copilot is showing selfies he just took sitting in the cockpit of the old Liberator.

Finally, an engineer and a mechanic arrive, disappearing into our plane and reappearing on top of it. There is much going back and forth to their tool bin and stock of parts. Every thirty minutes or so, they run the engines for a test, then turn them off and shake their heads.

The hours go by.

By late afternoon, the worst is realized. The plane is going nowhere. A part in the hydraulic system is not available, and they cannot jerry-rig a substitute. Another plane is flying in with the part, but it will not be able to take us to Tufi because it is getting dark and Tufi has no runway lights. So we are going back to Port Moresby. The next day is a Tuesday, when they do not fly to Tufi. This means losing two days from our trek of the villages on the coast around Tufi, reputed to be the most beautiful part of our tour. We have now been in Popondetta for ten hours.

Our practice of "going with the flow" has lost its charm at this point. We call Emanuel and ask him to tell his boss that the airline should be persuaded to schedule a Tuesday flight to Tufi from Port Moresby. Some hours later, we succeed: the airline has agreed to schedule the Tuesday flight. We further insist that all the people who waited in Popondetta with us be called and offered priority seating on that flight.

The next morning, we fly to Tufi without incident, with several other New Guineans whom we had befriended during the long wait.

Angorogho and the Skull Cave

The Tufi coast is a large bump on the northeastern nose of Papua New Guinea, jutting out into the Solomon Sea. It was formed eons ago when three local volcanoes erupted. The lava flow took the form of many long fingers pushing into the sea, creating long, narrow, steep-sided bays of calm water between the fingers. These bays are called "rias" by geographers and "fjords" by everybody else. The coast has white sandy beaches, crystalline waters, pristine coral beds, towering palm trees, rain forest, and a dozen villages.

There is one resort in the tiny town of Tufi Station, called, appropriately, Tufi Resort. It is high-end but very eco-conscious and encourages its clients to stay in village guesthouses. After lunch at the resort, we climb into a large outboard for the one-hour trip to the village of Angorogho on Afati Bay, the starting point for our trek in Tufi. On the way, we stop in a small village to pick up Clarence, who will be our guide on the peninsula.

As we approach Angorogho, a sing-sing group comes out to meet us and, behind them, the whole village. Their sing-sing outfits are similar to those we have seen, but the headdresses are a wild rainbow of bird of paradise feathers—red, yellow, blue, black, and

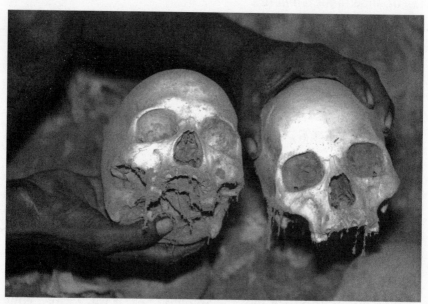

Skull Cave, Angorogho, Tufi

white, tied around the forehead and similar in shape to the classic Sioux chief's bonnet.

A path runs from the village to a point overlooking the sea. We arrive in time to see an enormous school of dolphin swim into shallow water near the beach, their backs glistening in the late afternoon sun as they roll through the still surface of the sea.

Before dinner, we climb into a dugout outrigger two-man canoe and cross Afati Bay to a mangrove swamp. Forty feet up on a cliff face are the Skull Caves where, one hundred years ago, the losing members of a warring tribe hid from the enemy and starved to death. A young man in a canoe, paddling furiously, catches up with us, hands something to Clarence, and paddles off. Clarence says, "It's about time. I needed this." Then he pops it in his mouth, and I realize this is a betel nut delivery.

We beach the canoe and clamber over slippery mangrove roots to get to the cliff, which is nearly vertical and crisscrossed with vines. With the assistance of our village escorts, one pulling from above and the other pushing from below, we scramble up the vines and footholds to the caves. Sure enough, there they are, four human skulls in one cave and two more in another. The villagers are fairly casual about handling the skulls, and Barbara takes pictures with their permission. We leave the skulls the way we found them, facing the cave entrances, perhaps still hoping for a delivery of bananas.

After dark, dinner is served in a ten-by-ten-foot open pavilion with bench seats and a thatched roof. The table is beautifully set, with traditional cloths and flower petals. The village chief, Donald, is our host. We are also joined by Clarence, Donald's sons and wife, and assorted villagers. We talk into the night. Donald brings out a coffee-table picture book about Tufi in which he, his family, and various people we have met are featured. He is proud of the sympathetic light in which Tufi is pictured but is disappointed that its publication has not led to further tourist interest.

31

The Angorogho guesthouse, where we stay that night, is a large thatched hut on stilts with four rooms at the seaside end of the village. Comfortable sleeping pads, pillows, and mosquito netting are provided.

We had previously misplaced our walking sticks before we left Brooklyn and ask Donald if one of the villagers could cut a couple of straight trimmed branches for us. The next morning, at breakfast, Donald presents us each with a polished hardwood stick, a taller one carved at the top in the figure of a man with a hat and a shorter one carved as a smiling woman with her hair in a topknot. He had stayed up much of the night fashioning the sticks. We were so touched by his generosity that we carried them home, overcoming hassles with the airlines.

Kwafururu and Tumari

We say good-bye and good luck to Donald, his family, and the rest of the villagers, who have gathered under a spreading tree in the center square and we begin our trek to Tumari Point with Clarence, his wife, two young daughters, and two cousins, one also named Donald. The hiking is strenuous, with a lot of steep ups and downs in the rain forest, slippery footing, and long stretches through high kunai grass. Midway through the trek, we pass through the village of Kwafururu.

The villagers have been expecting us (the single exception to the long list of modern appliances that the New Guineans don't own is the cellular phone, which they use to great convenience), and once again we are greeted and surrounded by a sing-sing group of extraordinary vivacity, led by the village elders. The footwork is especially intricate. The villagers have constructed a palm frond gate through which we pass into the village square, where we are "attacked" by a costumed and painted warrior wielding a seven-foot spear. Barbara takes pictures while I collapse on a canopied platform. I have lunch with Phillip, one of the elders in costume, who has been trained as a nurse. Dozens of village children come to see the *waitman*, the Tok Pisin lingo for *white man*. After lunch, villagers bestow upon us beautiful necklaces of cowrie shells and sing-sing us off into the bush, where we pick up our trek to Tumari.

An hour later, we reach the contact point on the shore and board outrigger dugout canoes paddled by Tumari villagers. Two paddlers move each canoe steadily against a stiff easterly wind. Tufi Coast villagers can paddle an outrigger for hours. They learn to paddle about the time they learn to walk. They have their own canoe by age five and are taught how to build one not long after. The dugout canoes are narrow so that the paddlers can place their feet one behind the other. There is a four-by-four-foot deck lashed onto the middle of the craft for supplies or passengers. The outrigger ensures a very smooth, swift ride.

Sitting on the deck and leaning back against my pack, I enjoy the scenery and fall asleep. I awake as we approach the beach landing for Tumari village. It is late afternoon. We wade in and are welcomed by a delegation who escort us to the village center. We are seated on chairs in the middle of a clearing and adorned with leis of white frangipani flowers. The guesthouse is still under construction, but the village has a large pavilion in the middle of the village green—a raised, roofed platform, with open sides. It is used for various village activities, for guest accommodations, and for villagers to hang out in. In the very center of the platform is a tent of mosquito netting with some sleeping pads, pillows, and covers. "That's us," I say.

By now, it is dark, and having reconnoitered the village's latrine and a hastily screened-off bathing spot complete with wash tub and ladle, we take a bucket bath, change clothes, and have dinner on the platform while being attended to by ten or twelve villagers who chat and ask questions. A white-crested cockatoo, the size of a chicken, lands abruptly on the platform next to us and looks us over. The villagers laugh and reach out to pet him, obviously a semidomesticated bird.

Discussion with the villagers continues into the night. They talk about farming, tourism, religion, families, and fishing, both here and in the US. An important fishing event is the annual tuna run in which an entire shoal of tuna—thousands of them—come around the point and stop in the cove of the Tumari bay for several days, sometimes weeks. The villagers accept this as nature's bounty and deploy nets every day during the run to take in hundreds of fish, a mere dent in the shoal. Many are eaten shortly after the day of the catch, but most are cleaned and smoked to provide the village with needed protein for the rest of the year.

Finally, we beg off to retire to our gauzy chamber. Several small groups linger, chatting, laughing, and singing late into the night until they fall asleep elsewhere on the platform. As I drift off to sleep, I think about the diminutive tuna scout in Wewak and wonder if he has scouted Tufi. I hope not.

In the morning, Phillip, a Tumari elder, joins our group as we set out from Tumari on the final leg of our trek to Kwafundi Bay. The trek culminates in our predicament on the lava rock cliff above Koruwe Bay, where we skirt the edge with the sheer drop and attempt to descend.

The squeal of a pig jolts me out of my musings as it races along the top of the cliff. I fear for a moment that young Donald, who is carrying me, will drop his cargo, get his spear, and chase the pig. It turns out to be a domestic pig that had gotten out of its pen. It bolts away, chased by a dog and followed closely by its owner.

We overcome the obstacles of the shrub in the trail by main force, with Donald and Clarence lifting me over the bush. The rest of the descent is less tricky as the cliff slopes outward. Shortly after we reach level ground, Barbara expresses relief at finishing in one piece and promptly slips on loose stones, falling on her rear end.

Nothing hurts except her dignity. Clarence's wife and daughters come skipping down behind us, having negotiated the cliff face with enviable ease.

Our hike ends at Koruwe Bay, where we board a waiting outrigger canoe. It glides swiftly over the calm waters of the bay, but when it turns the corner out of the bay into the open sea, the wind rises and whitecaps appear. The paddlers work hard for two hours. Clarence and Phillip go ashore and walk along the shingle to ease the load and allow a shallower draft so the canoe can run close to the beach where the headwind diminishes.

Finally, we reach Kwafurina Bay and, once again on calm water, the outrigger skims the surface, headed for Banafe Island. The canoe glides over live coral reefs that coil and uncoil in the current like so many heads of Medusa, showing colors of magenta, gold, and, of course, coral. Our bow paddler says there are many lobster beds in the Bay, and I long to tear off my clothes and swim among the creatures of this glistening silence—but there is no time. Tomorrow, the boat will come to return us to Tufi Resort, and then we will travel by plane to Port Moresby for the long flight home. The day for diving was lost at Popondetta, though it was a day gained in hanging out with the New Guineans.

We circle the island, which doesn't take long. It is a little more than one hundred yards long and fifty yards wide, shaped like a loaf of bread, rising steeply about fifty feet out of the water. As we circle, we see, silhouetted against the sky, feathered headdresses of the Kwafundi dancers. We approach the small dock at the end of the island as they begin their chant of welcome: "*Oro. Oro. Oro.*"

The path from the dock is steep and it takes a few minutes to stretch our old bones after the long canoe ride. The singers and dancers escort us to the lovely hut on stilts where we will stay. We meet the Chief, Smith, his wife, Ethel, and their extended family. The whole Kwafundi clan has turned up for the occasion, but only Smith and

Ethel and their immediate family live on the island. There isn't room for anyone else. The rest live on the hillsides of the bay.

Smith and Ethel join us for dinner. We talk with Smith about Tufi, the island, and tourism. Except for a small patch on the island, all of the clan's gardens are on the mainland. Smith calls it Smith Island, since his family has been its only inhabitants for eighteen years. He built huts and planted gardens and all the trees. Before they arrived, it was just an uninhabited mound covered with kunai grass. Ethel, who does not speak English, smiles.

Smith also built four guesthouses, which an Australian developer promised would be filled. But no tourists came. The developer died, and his heirs were uninterested in the venture. The guest huts crumbled from disuse and disrepair. But, at the urging of the Tufi Resort and Ecotourism, the agency that arranged our trip, Smith rebuilt two guesthouses. We are the first tourists to visit.

In the morning, we pack our trekking gear and get ready for our motorboat pick-up from Tufi Resort. The entire extended family comes from the bayside to see us off. Clarence's wife bids us a tearful good-bye. She and Barbara have bonded, despite the fact that they don't speak a common language.

I walk to the end of the island and look north up the bay toward the sea. The water is as still as a forest pond. Three children, on their way to school in their outriggers, dart across the bay like water bugs. I turn to take in the whole view—swaying coconut palms; black lava-rock cliffs with dark mangrove swamps at their base and rain forest at their summit; green mountain peaks rising out of the morning fog; beached dugout canoes; small groups of thatched huts near the shore, each bordered by a garden of orchids. I wonder if this will look the same in ten years. In five years. In one year.

But I have seen this. I have been here and will go back, if not in fact, then in memory.

The outboard arrives with William, the supervising guide at Tufi. He is anxious to verify that we are, as represented on numerous cellphone calls he has made throughout the trip, alive and whole. We sit in the back of the open boat, draped in oilskins, and head for the ocean. The craft slices through the calm bay waters for a few minutes, then bangs its way for an hour through six-foot waves on the sea. It spends half its time in the air as does my sore butt, which slams down on a metal seat with every bound. We reach the Resort inlet, and the torment subsides.

During our lunch with the resort manager, a hornbill, a cricket bat–sized beak masquerading as a bird, lands on our table looking for scraps. It is, apparently, a regular guest. We are able to take a brief rest and shower before the assistant manager drives us to the landing strip, which begins at the water's edge and ends a few hundred yards inland at a sand dune. The plane coming in looks like it is going to surf the last few yards, but it lands smoothly on the tarmac. It is time to say good-bye.

On one of the stops on the way to Port Moresby, four fully-costumed, painted, and feathered sing-sing dancers board the plane. Their bonnets, made with bird of paradise feathers, are too tall for the window seats so they have to sit on the aisle. As they change seats, their ankle shells rattle.

The trek is over.

Afterthoughts

What did we find in Papua New Guinea? A beautiful country, with dramatic mountain ranges swathed in deep-green rain forest, and a profusion of exotic multicolored orchids, lilies, roses, and other rare flora. We also found a beautiful people—generous, hardworking, and proud of their culture.

Papua New Guinea is a country at a significant crossroad. It may become just another third-world country tied to the juggernaut of the global economy, with foreign private investment financing poorly regulated, exploitative, and environmentally degrading mining, logging, and fishing industries, facilitated by corrupt elected officials. Some might say this is inevitable: the country cannot advance without foreign investment. Who else will build the infrastructure (roads, railways, mine shafts, oil drills) necessary to lift New Guinea into the modern world of consumption, which everybody wants?

Or does everybody? The reason for New Guinea's historically slow development—its geography and stable subsistence economy—may be the factors that enable the country to successfully resist such inevitabilities. The people have developed ways of life that are stable, relatively healthy, and aesthetically satisfying, relying solely on their own wits, the renewable resources in the bush around them, and a mutually supportive social structure. Unlike the peoples of many of the newly minted third-world countries with extensive colonial histories, the New Guineans we spoke to did not appear to aspire to the economic and social status of former colonists. They would like more schools and health clinics and some modest sources of income, but they are not starving; they have shelter and beautiful surroundings. And they have patience.

They have the space and time to develop their resources themselves—or not.

Many of the young New Guineans we met have no intention of leaving their villages.

They know what has happened to their colleagues who have disappeared into Port Moresby slums. Even though they are fluent in standard English and familiar with auto engines, outboard motors, and iPhones, they will stay home.

Will they remain passive if their way of life is threatened? Will the Tumari villagers look the other way if the Spanish trawlers come for their tuna? I don't think so.

Algeria:

Why Algeria?

Algeria is, after all, a repressive police state facing a militant Islamic opposition movement. It is on the State Department Travel Advisory List, and there are almost no foreign tourists.

So, why Algeria? Because it has a beautiful Mediterranean coastline and a lush coastal plain; a countryside studded with the ruins of Roman cities; Arab, Berber, and African cultures; the Great Erg, the Sahara's sea of sand; the Tuareg-inhabited South; the M'zab culture of the East; and Algiers, with its Casbah, corniche, harbor, seafood, couscous, and French urban design and architecture.

And because it has a lengthy and heroic history of resistance to colonization that inspired anticolonial revolutionary movements throughout the third world.

There are also almost no foreign tourists.

When visiting Algeria, you have to take some chances and be ready to operate out of your comfort zone. Algerian tourism is not ready for prime time, but prime time isn't ready for Algeria, either.

Habibi and Mr. Cool

Friday, October 7, 2011, is a very pleasant day in Brooklyn for our departure, with temperatures in the low seventies. Barbara and I do a light workout and go through the pack list. The cab driver to JFK International Airport is Palestinian, and we engage in a lengthy conversation about Jerusalem, where his family lives, and Gaza, where we had visited with a UN-sponsored delegation in 2009.

We arrive at JFK in plenty of time for our 3:40 p.m. flight. The Lufthansa check-in attendant issues boarding passes, then looks at our passports for an inordinate amount of time, her face gradually assuming an expression of concern.

"Wait a moment. I need to talk to my supervisor about something," she says and walks off with our passports. They include our visas, which we had obtained weeks before from the Algerian Embassy in Washington, DC. My sense of well-being vanishes and is replaced by the needle-stick onset of anxiety. Time goes by. When she reappears, her expression is unchanged.

"We can't let you board. There is a problem with Dennis's visa. The expiration date is August 23, 2011." I look. She's right. It is clearly a typographical error, since the date of issue is also August 23, 2011, and this visa is good for ninety days. The Embassy clerk must have absent-mindedly retyped the issuance date on the expiration date line. We all agree with this explanation, but the airline would be fined if they let me board with an expired date on a visa.

I ask to see her supervisor. Minutes later, a tall, slender, impeccably suited African American man comes up to us. He is Mr. Cool, soft-spoken, exquisitely courteous, calm, and ever so slightly bemused. But he is adamant—I cannot board with the visa as is. He hints at a solution. The error can be corrected by the issuing entity. A suitable letter from the Embassy, admitting the error, faxed to his office, would suffice. Within seconds, I am on the phone with

41

Rita, the travel agent in Seattle who had made the visa arrangements and with whom we have done much business. Fortunately, she is in the office. Within seconds, she is on another phone to the Algerian Embassy. I can hear her side of the conversation, which is in Arabic. I hear her repeat one of the five or six words I understand, *habibi*. *Sweetheart.* They break off for Habibi to draft a letter on Embassy stationary. Many calls are made, and Habibi keeps saying he will fax the letter momentarily.

By now, the flight is boarding, the stress is mounting, and Mr. Cool keeps checking the fax machine but there is nothing from Habibi. Barbara leans on the counter and holds her head. I pace back and forth. Silently, I recite the traveler's mantra, "Roll with the punches." I think, *Is there a later flight? If so, what is the ripple effect on our connection in Frankfurt? On our accommodations in Algiers?* More calls are made. Finally, at 3:10 p.m. the fax comes through and Mr. Cool springs into action. Moving like a gazelle, he whisks us past all the passport and ticket checkpoints and through Homeland Security, shucking his shoes and jacket like everybody else. We arrive at the gate with two minutes to spare. He smiles and nods politely as we thank him and stagger into the 747, carrying all our gear, stunned by this narrow escape from an early trip implosion. *Ma Salaama.* Good-bye, Mr. Cool.

Algiers and Sidi of the North

Twelve hours later, on Saturday, October 8, we land in Algiers. We are greeted by Sidi, who will be our guide and driver for most of our trip. In Tamanrasset, in the deep South, we will have another guide named Sidi. So I refer to them as Sidi of the North (Sidi N) and Sidi of the South (Sidi S).

Sidi N is an affable but tough sixty-eight-year-old Arabic grandfather with five children and many grandchildren, the oldest of whom is eighteen. He speaks excellent English, French, and some of the Berber dialects. Sidi N knows everyone and everyone knows him, a great asset in our travels. He is resourceful, responsible, and caring. At the same time, he is casually racist, misogynist, and reactionary—a walking contradiction. He denigrates the hygiene and work habits of the "blacks" from Niger; yet, when he meets a Nigerien whom he knows, they immediately embrace and he praises them to us. He speaks disapprovingly of female drivers yet abhors the restrictions imposed on women by Islamic fundamentalists. He disparages the Palestinians as troublemakers yet identifies intensely with the Algerian struggle for independence from France. His strongest pejorative is calling someone a "vagabond," which, we infer, he equates with "bum."

Algiers looks like a shopworn Paris. The major streets are broad and curve gracefully over and around the city's hills. They are lined with whitewashed fin de siècle buildings resembling those of the Ile de La Cité in Paris. The city forms a crescent that embraces the Bay of Algiers. Its white hills tumble down to the sea. A corniche runs erratically along the waterfront, from which one can watch the busy harbor traffic—container ships, freighters, tugs, Navy gunboats, car ferries, and the fishing fleet. No cruise ships.

Our hotel, the Safir, like most, was built by the French. It has a kind of oddball elegance, a combination of art deco and French period furnishings and two balky open-faced elevators. Our room on the fourth floor has a balcony that overlooks the harbor, compensating for the erratic plumbing and frayed white and pink Louis XV furniture. We wander into the third-floor dining room to claim our prepaid dinner, only to find it dark and vacant. I rouse a pot cleaner in the kitchen who says it opens at seven p.m., which is the time on my watch. It takes a few minutes for me to realize that I've gained two time zones since Frankfurt and that it's only five p.m. in Algiers. Later, we have an excellent fish dinner with a half-bottle of Coteaux de Mascara, a sturdy Algerian Cabernet. It's a pleasant surprise to get wine in Islamic Algeria.

Wine, which cannot be found throughout the rest of the country, is available only in Algiers. However, the food we encounter everywhere is delicious. A typical Algerian meal consists of couscous, vegetables, and, occasionally, mutton, goat, or fish.

Algeria in a Nutshell

Algeria is home to thirty-five million people—99 percent are Arab or Berber and 1 percent is European. The predominant religion is Sunni Islam. Algeria is the largest country in Africa, with vast natural gas and oil reserves and virtually no national debt. It is also agriculturally self-sufficient because of its extremely fertile and productive coastal plain. The government provides free education, medical care, subsidized housing, and basic welfare support for the unemployed.

From 1954 until 1962, the country endured a bloody war for independence from France, during which an estimated one million Algerians were slain. The FLN (National Liberation Front) veterans who led the fight have run the country since and been accused of the crony corruption that so often accompanies unchecked power. When Islamic parties won local elections and were poised to win national elections, the results were nullified and elections canceled by the ruling party, which was also backed by the military. This led, in 1992, to a ten-year civil war, during which atrocities were committed by both sides. The exhausted belligerents finally agreed to a cease-fire and amnesty in 2002, and there has been relative quiet since, with the occasional bombing or tourist abduction.

Police presence is pervasive. There are "controls" (checkpoints) on the highways, back roads, and all over the cities, causing massive traffic jams. Most checks involve cursory look-ins. With Sidi N at the wheel, we generally sail through. But if the driver or vehicle is not well known, or the occupants of the car don't have their ID papers in order, or the officer in charge just feels like it, the vehicle is emptied and searched.

The development of tourism is a low priority. The government invests in its biggest cash cow, fossil fuel, and that means most development money goes south where highways, fully subsidized housing developments, manufacturing facilities, schools, and universities are being built in the sparsely populated Sahara to help exploit the country's natural resources. As a result, Algiers's corniche, museums, parks, metro, boulevards, bridges, and buildings are pretty much as the French left them in 1962, though deteriorated through neglect. The streets are full of unemployed young men, each claiming a particular stairway or wall as his hangout. The money and the jobs are in the South, and in the maintenance of a huge security apparatus.

Although few Algerians speak English, most speak French. They tend to speak more slowly than Parisians, enabling us to engage in simple conversations.

The Casbah

The day after we arrive, we drive to the Casbah, the oldest part of Algiers, dating back to the Ottoman era. It sits on a hill of its own and occupies only a few square kilometers. Twenty thousand people live in the Casbah, most families occupying only one room. Toilets are communal, with one per eighteen residents, and water is obtained from a tap in the street. Food is cooked over bottled gas in the doorway of the family's room.

In bad shape to begin with, the Casbah was heavily damaged by an earthquake in 2003. The ruined dwellings are not being replaced but torn down, their sites converted to tiny parks or public squares. The government is relocating a few hundred residents each year to newer housing on the edge of the city, with electricity, running water,

Entrance to the Casbah, Algiers

and interior toilets, though some resist leaving the homes of their ancestors and the conspiratorial intimacy of the Casbah.

Venturing into the Casbah alone is not a good idea for outsiders. It is honeycombed with alleys, stairways, tunnels, and one-meter lanes where the sun never shines. Signage is negligible. Even police are reluctant to go into it by themselves.

At an entry point near the summit of the hill stands Dar Mustapha Pacha, a graceful, small palace, whitewashed and dark-timbered, with a central courtyard and fountain. This was the residence of the Ottoman deys of Algiers until the French invaded in 1830. Next to it is a low building with barred windows that looks like a jail from a Hollywood Western set. Appropriately, it is the local police station. The station commanders do not look happy to see us and Sidi N has to jolly them up for twenty minutes or so before they grudgingly agree to let us descend into their infamous precinct. They insist that a policeman accompany us.

We start our journey going up a gradually sloping lane about three meters wide that soon narrows to two and begins tunneling and twisting its way through and between the aging stucco walls. There are few people, just darting figures briefly glimpsed through doorways. But thirty minutes later, when we come upon a tiny open space formed by the intersection of three lanes and an empty lot, several men are apparently waiting to see us. Even here, people know Sidi N and greet him with much embracing and cheek-kissing. They smile and wave to us, already aware that two American tourists were coming through the Casbah. "The Arab Telephone," explains Sidi N.

Meanwhile, the young policeman in jeans and a T-shirt who had accompanied us has disappeared. "Maybe he got bored," says Sidi N.

The FLN resistance in Algiers was based in the Casbah. The police station where the insurgents were tortured is now vacant. Pontecorvo's film, *The Battle of Algiers*, was shot here. As we make our way down the other side of the Casbah we see a few tiny shops— shoe repair, tailor, tinsmith—scarcely wider than their doorways. There is also a *haman*, a communal bath, used by men in the morning and women in the afternoon. When women are using the bath, a pink towel is hung across the entryway.

Outside the Casbah

We emerge from the Casbah into a bustling street market, then cross a street to a seaside Ottoman fortress. It is vacant except for a small suite of rooms, about the size of an average Starbucks, hidden behind an unmarked door. A little old man sitting in an aging swivel chair in a windowless room presides over the "archives" of the war for independence. He is giddy with delight at our visit, probably the first by foreigners in years. Discovering that I have read Frantz Fanon, seen *The Battle of Algiers*, and know something about that struggle, he is in rapture.

The archives consist of hundreds of paper boxes, one for each prominent insurgent or martyr, hand labeled and filled with documents, photos, and yellowed newspaper clippings. Pictures of the heroes cover every inch of the walls. The curator speaks no English but happily holds forth in French while Sidi N tries to keep up with the translation. Waist-high stacks of old newspapers fill an adjacent small alcove. A few military artifacts—a gas mask, a grenade, some bullets—lie in a glass-fronted bookcase. He gives us little Algerian flags. When we leave, he shakes our hands warmly, very pleased that someone else in the world is interested in the events that are the focal point of his life.

As rare solo tourists, we elicit stares wherever we go; as Americans, astonished exclamations; and as New Yorkers, smiles and nods. It is as if the third anomaly explains the first two. Very few Algerians speak English, but we often hear the phrase, *Welcome to Algeria*. Barbara takes many close-up photographs of people on the street. Her openness and smiles generate enthusiasm, and when she shows her subjects the photographs she has taken on the camera's review screen, they burst into laughter.

We end the day at the Jardin d'Essai, a huge public botanical garden with an impressive central avenue of palms, a tropical pond, and species of trees from all over Algeria. However, the gate is closed. Sidi N importunes a passing groundskeeper to let us in, invoking our status as the US's entire tourist contingent to Algeria for 2011. The gate opens, and we have the place to ourselves. We walk the paths, admiring the lush greenery, then sit near the pond till late afternoon, soaking in its atmosphere of quiet beauty and contemplation.

On Monday, we check out and drive up one of Algiers's higher hills to Notre Dame d'Afrique, a small, lovely church in the Byzantine style. It holds ecumenical services for Christians, Muslims, and Jews and overlooks the old synagogue, the Jewish cemetery, and the sea. We attempt to visit the cemetery, but the gate is locked, so Sidi N reprises the Jardin routine. The gate opens. The cemetery is vast, the largest in Algiers. However, the living Jewish community in Algeria is decimated. At one time, it numbered in the tens of thousands, a vibrant, productive population well integrated with its Sunni Muslim neighbors. The combination of Muslim resentment of French favoritism toward Jews, antipathy generated by Israeli oppression of the Palestinians, and the rise of a particularly aggressive version of Islamic fundamentalism has reduced the Algerian Jewish population to less than five thousand. The cemetery has been neglected, if not vandalized. Many graves and mausoleums are broken open and empty. There are few stones of remembrance on the gravesites. The latest dates we saw on tombstones were in the eighties. It is a melancholy and desolate place.

The Martyrs, Monument is on a hilltop overlooking Algiers. Ninety-two meters high, the swooping concrete abstraction was built by the Canadian government in 1982 to honor the Algerians killed in the war of independence. The monument dominates the skyline and can be seen from almost any point in and around the city.

Nearby is the Museum of the Armed Forces, which Sidi N is very eager for us to see. The museum's dioramas present the history of Algeria as an endless series of battles between indigenous North Africans and foreign invaders, from the Phoenicians to the Romans to the French. It makes the point that there was continual armed resistance to the French occupation—the defense by the Dey of Algiers at the time of the invasion in 1830, the insurgency led by Amir Abdel Kader in the mid-1800s, the die-hard holdout of the Tuareg in the South until the 1920s, the formation of FLN in the 1950s. Sidi N is intensely interested in each of the exhibits and comments on all of them, especially those of the final successful war of independence. One of these is a scale model of French paratroopers throwing bound Algerians off a high bridge in Constantine. Sidi N adds that French police threw insurgents captured in Paris into the Seine.

Among the things we don't see in Algiers are traffic lights, motorcycles, panhandlers, dogs, and, of course, Americans.

Tamanrasset, the Tuareg, and Sidi of the South

After a two-and-a–half-hour night flight, we land in Tamanrasset, the southernmost city of any size in Algeria. Tamanrasset is almost the same distance from Algiers as is London, England. We are met at the airport by two men in traditional Tuareg dress, one of whom holds a sign reading DENNIS DUANE JAMES. He welcomes us, introducing himself as our guide, Sidi. The other man is Khan, our driver, a large fellow who speaks Arabic, French, and Berber, but no English. It becomes painfully clear within a few minutes after we get in their Toyota 4x4 Land Cruiser that Sidi S has a very tenuous grasp of English. A frisson of paranoia quickens my heart. *Who are these guys?* I picture our real guide and driver, bound and gagged (or worse) in some dank cellar, where we are to be similarly restrained while our captors demand ransom in lieu of our decapitation.

I ask questions only the real guide would be likely to know: the name of the travel agency, our itinerary in Tamanrasset, our US city of origin. Sidi S's answers are non-sequiturs. Khan stares glumly into the desolate darkness. My paranoia shifts into high gear. Just then the 4x4 pulls into a driveway and stops at a sky-blue gate marked Garden of Outoul, the designated accommodation in our travel packet. Hoping my sigh of relief is not too noticeable, I downshift my anxiety level to the mundane problem of how we're going to deal with the language barrier over the next few days. We are escorted to a garden apartment among twenty or so, all vacant, in a villa situated in an orchard.

The next morning, Barbara and I walk around the walled property, which covers two or three acres, taking in the fruit trees, peacocks roaming free, and a penned enclosure for tiny deer. Our destination for the next two days is Assekrem, a jagged mountain on a high volcanic plateau of the Hoggar Range, seventy-three kilometers into the desert. After some delay because of reports of high winds and flooding in the mountains, we set off. The "road" to Assekrem is a *piste*—a French word for a track or trail. That's all there is, and in many areas the track has been washed out by the recent rains, and only a gully remains. Khan slowly but skillfully negotiates around these obstacles, sometimes going at the pace of a slow walk for hundreds of meters. For six hours, we lurch, lunge, wallow, and jounce our way up into the plateau.

The landscape is awesome. Rocks the size of cathedrals and mesas like a giant's table rise straight up out of the desert. Camels, goats, and burros appear in groups, seemingly without attendants. A Tuareg, riding a white camel and leading three others, appears in the far distance. The rider wears an indigo-blue robe. His loose *tagelmust* (head covering) covers all but his eyes. Transfixed, we watch him approach. He greets Khan, obliges his mount to kneel, and, barefoot, adroitly climbs down from his saddle, using the camel's neck as a step. He and Khan chat and we exchange greetings before he climbs back up his camel and his tiny caravan ambles back into the desert.

Tuareg, Tamanrasset

The Tuareg are a nomadic people who live in the heart of the Sahara in southern Algeria and Libya and northern Mali, Niger, and Mauretania. They raise and trade sheep, goats, and camels. Additionally, they are fierce warriors. They know the desert like no one else and move freely across national borders, riding their distinctive white camels. The Tuareg are nominally Muslim. The men typically wear blue robes and tagelmusts. The women decorate their hands with henna and do not cover their faces. Some Tuareg have settled in towns or cities and become expert silversmiths, exporting their wares to Europe and the United States. Those who remain nomadic have been known to engage in a little smuggling, and some hire out as mercenaries.

Later, another Tuareg appears, walking alone across the trackless expanse. The same tableau ensues, after which he continues his walk until he disappears into the distance.

Sunset, Sunrise

Finally, in the early evening, our 4x4 grinds up a narrow, steep grade to the Refuge, a large stone building that constitutes a hostel for pilgrims such as we. The only other visitors are a Catalan couple and a woman from Lyon, with their respective guides and drivers. Barbara and I get a room to ourselves. After dire warnings from Sidi S about the strenuous nature of the climb and questions regarding our heart conditions, we set off for the summit of Assekrem. It is a piece of cake, a well-marked gradual switchback that gets us on top in thirty minutes. The plateau below, pierced by cones, arches, and mesas, extends to the horizon and is a spectrum of reds, from dusty rose to blood orange. As the sun sets, shadows and clouds compete in a race to change color, inventing both subtle and dramatic hues undreamed of by Benjamin Moore.

At a height of twenty-eight hundred meters, the wind cuts through my light jacket. Near the summit is a stone hut once used by the esthete monk Charles Eugène de Foucauld. I shelter behind its entryway, watching the light show until I am thoroughly chilled, then head down in the near darkness.

We learn from the Catalan couple's guide that de Foucauld (1858–1916) was a French Vicomte and notorious roué who, in his late twenties, wandered North Africa, had a spiritual awakening, was ordained a priest, and founded a monastic order based in Tamanrasset. He eschewed any luxury, ate only dates and barley, and attracted a following of one. His life's work was to translate the bible into Tamashek, the Tuareg language. Later, he was shot to death in Tamanrasset by a Tuareg who believed he was helping the French Army infiltrate Tuareg villages.

When the guide is out of earshot, one of the Catalans tells us he is a journalist. "I did not put that information on my visa application," he says. "If I had, I would never have been allowed to enter the country." For our applications, we had disclosed that we are attorneys and that I also write. "A writer is as threatening to the government as a journalist," he tells us. "Don't mention that on any visa application."

The night is very cold. We strip the four empty bunks in our room of their covers and pile them on top of us.

The next morning, we get up early to see the sunrise from the top of Assekrem. It is another fantasy in red, the eastern faces of the brooding mesas and grotesque crags suddenly glowing like lanterns while their shadows stretch out and then draw back behind them, as if someone had opened a Gate of Hell and was now slowly pulling it shut.

The Artists, the Monk, the Queen, and the Chief

On the drive back to Tamanrasset, Barbara asks Sidi S about Neolithic pictographs that are supposed to be in the vicinity of our route. He smiles and says, "Tomorrow, tomorrow," which has been his answer for the last two days. When I ask if he knows where they are, he gives a vague answer. It's clear he doesn't know anything about the drawings or doesn't understand what we're asking—or both. While Barbara fumes, I piece together an inquiry in French to Khan. His face lights up, "*Oui, oui. Bien sûr.*" Minutes later, the 4x4 is rocketing down a wadi, a dry riverbed.

In about half an hour, Khan pulls up, and there, ten meters away, are the drawings, mostly of animals and people, covering at least four square meters of standing red rock. They overlap and have differing degrees of verisimilitude to the creatures portrayed: obvious figures of humans, camels, snakes, and scorpions; and less obvious representations of horses and cattle. Most are stick figures, but some have carefully rendered features. Farther down the wadi are more pictographs clustered on high rising rocks on the sides of the dry streambed. There is no official signage, no explanatory material. We are alone with the doodles of our species from two to ten thousand years ago. Were these religious icons? Tribal signs? Journal entries? Or just something to do at the riverside while waiting for the wash to dry? The pictures are in the open, not in a cave. We acknowledge the artists' wish that they be seen, collection by collection, like gallery hopping in Chelsea. Finally, an hour and many photos later, we leave the site to its mysterious purpose. What profundity do we take with us? Not much. Just more evidence of the uniquely human impulse to transcend our brief existence with art.

In Tamanrasset, we again stumble upon one of Charles de Foucauld's former dwellings while browsing through shops for Tuareg silverwork. It is a small, windowless mud hut in a compound that also encloses a one-room school for Tuareg children, a chapel, and a shop. Members of de Foucauld's order, a young French woman and a young Polish man, sell handmade Tuareg crafts to help support the school. They are proud of their work and spend thirty minutes telling us about de Foucauld and their mission. They're nice, and we hope they don't get shot like de Foucauld.

A short drive from Tamanrasset, just outside the oasis village of Abalessa, sit ruins and a small museum, which we visit the next day. Sidi S chats with the museum caretaker, ignoring the ruins. Khan, Barbara, and I nose around until we find a marker in French indicating that this was the residence, citadel, and tomb of Queen Tin Hinan. The tomb is empty. Sidi S, Khan, and the caretaker have no further information, and we learn nothing about the mysterious Queen. Once back in New York, we find out that she lived in the fourth century and was accorded great prestige as the matriarch of the Tuareg. It's strange that three Algerians living in a region populated by the Tuareg could not, or perhaps would not, tell us anything about this historic figure.

We leave the Queen's place to have lunch with a local family. Our host is the Tuareg chief of the village. He is a portly, stolid oligarch who barks orders to his sons and minions. He holds court under a large, leafy tree and serves us tea. We exhaust what few polite inquiries we have regarding his family, the village, and the weather, while he volunteers little and asks no questions in return. He has a substantial house into which we are not invited. The chief directs two of his sons, around eight and ten years old, to take Barbara and me on a tour of his property, which is several acres large, walled in, and planted with various productive crops and trees. Much of it is fodder for his herds of goats, but we also notice date palms, vegetables, and citrus trees. The boys are charming, quickly overcoming the language barrier by gesture and pantomime. They are delighted by Barbara's photos. They show us the water supply and distribution system—a well with a motorized pump and a maze of shallow trenches among the crops.

Lunch is served in a replica of a Tuareg nomad shelter within the chief's compound. The roof and walls are made of woven palm wood slats. The chief sleeps there every night on a palm wood pallet. After lunch, while Barbara takes pictures of the chief and his boys, I try the pallet and doze off, to everyone's amusement. Things further loosen up when the chief's wife brings out his youngest, a one-year-old son.

In the evening, we return to the Garden of Outoul hotel and retire early for our flight to Ghardia.

The M'zab

The old Air Algeria prop plane lands on the runway of the airport that services the M'zab Valley, in particular, the Mozambite cities of Ghardia, El Atteuf, Bou Nour, Melika, and Beni Isguen. The familiar figure of Sidi N in his trademark khaki bill cap and photographer's vest appears; he's as happy to see us as we are to see him. Word has already gotten back to him that the person assigned to us in the South as an English-speaking guide was neither, and he was worried. We assure him that Khan saved most of the day.

The Mozambites are a Berber people who practice an ultraorthodox version of Islam known as Ibadi. They were driven out of Northern Algeria by the Sunni Arab invasions and, beginning in the twelfth century AD, established five cities, each on a fortified hilltop above the M'zab Valley. They number 250,000, the largest concentration being 80,000 in Ghardia. They do not proselytize or use violence against nonbelievers. They are largely self-sufficient, having, over the centuries, devised unique methods of water supply and distribution. They are the shrewdest businessmen in Algeria, especially in the fields of retail sales and heavy construction, conducting business in locations throughout the country and abroad, and sending their profits home to the M'zab.

The cities are among the most graceful, architecturally, that we have ever seen, and that applies to both their old and new sections. The houses and streets are in perfect harmony with their environment. The buildings are whitewashed, with occasional pale-blue, soft-pink, or tan coloring, but are devoid of ornamentation. These dwellings have been designed to maximize comfort in the intense heat, with small windows, narrow outside lanes, and inner courtyards that provide shade. The principal mosque and fortress sits at the top of a hill with a square minaret beside it. From a distance, each town looks like a Cubist painting. The "new cities," which are privately developed extensions of the old, are built on the same model, but with more amenities. The seven-hundred-year-old Mosque of Sheik Sidi Brahim in El Atteuff, now seldom used, is a small, pure-white one-story building with sensuously curved walls and ingeniously divided interior space. It was an inspiration for Le Corbusier's design for several churches in France.

The community is prosperous. The cities are clean. Crime is minimal. No vagabonds are here.

Mosque of Sheik Sidi Brahim, El Atteuff

These are, however, cities of men. Young unmarried women, who are allowed to show their faces, pass us in the lanes. Then there are ghostly figures, shrouded in white and completely covered up with only one eye exposed, hugging the buildings as they hurry by. They are the married women. These one-eyed wraiths turn their faces away if the eye makes contact with a male eye from outside the family. And even these phantoms and their unmarried sisters disappear from the streets in the evening. Men seem to run everything. Marriages are arranged by men. Male elders govern the cities and resolve all disputes. Men control all the businesses.

Cultural or religious transgressions result in expulsion from the community, Sidi N tells us, shaking his head. He deplores these restrictions on women, but they seem to accept their situation—or at least show no obvious signs of rebellion. The population of M'zab is growing. There appears to be no mass exodus of women, and those who leave often come back. (Coincidentally, upon our return to the US, we see a new opera, *Dark Sister*, about the difficulty Mormon women have in walking away from their community.)

Tourist access to the residential streets is restricted. A local guide must be engaged. Photographs of the residents are prohibited. Access to the mosques is denied, except, occasionally, to that of Sheik Sidi Brahim.

The Mozambites don't need tourism. It is tolerated but not encouraged.

That is their right and, for them, it is probably a good policy. And who knows? Maybe behind those silent white walls, the women are running the show, telling the men, including the elders, what to do. But I don't think so.

Timimoun, the Sea of Sand

We drive 630 kilometers across scrub desert, from Ghardia to Timimoun, an oasis town on the edge of the Grand Erg Occidental, also known as the Sea of Sand. About halfway, we stop at the mining town of El Golea. There, in the cemetery adjoining the small Catholic Church of St. Joseph, is the tomb of Charles de Foucauld, the ascetic monk. We seem to have become his followers. The grave is a simple concrete sarcophagus with his name and dates of birth and death, with no crosses or weeping angels. I'm sure he would have approved.

We find a small museum of natural history nearby. When we walk in to have a look, the young director is so excited he nearly has a stroke. He takes us through all the exhibits and, from memory, explains every dinosaur bone, arrowhead, lance point, cutting tool, grindstone, stew pot, and stuffed bird in the place. The museum is lovingly maintained and very interesting. Miners turn up a lot of old items and bring them to him. However, funding is scarce. We make his day, and, perhaps, his year.

We arrive at Timimoun in the early evening. It is a small, pretty town of eighteen thousand, sometimes called the Red Oasis because of the red clay used to make the stucco for its buildings. The Sudanese architecture of the city is particularly striking and uniform, consisting of deep-red walls with cream trim and crenellation. The main street, First of November Avenue, is a wide boulevard lined with shops, markets, cafés, hotels, and government buildings. It is a lively thoroughfare traversed by a wide variety of peoples—Arabs, Berbers, Sudanese, Nigeriens, Malinese, Mauretanians, a few Europeans, and two Americans. It is a treat just to sit in an outdoor café on the avenue, mentally translating a daily *Liberté* or *El Watan* newspaper, and watching this colorful parade.

Later, we stroll through the marketplace. The vendors are very friendly, and Barbara's pictures of them elicit loud guffaws. Due to all our walking, the sole of one of her light hikers has separated. People direct us to a shoe repair facility in the market, where we find a young man with a small carpet, some tools, cans of polish, and a manual sewing machine. He fixes the boot in ten minutes and charges the equivalent of fifty cents. The repair lasts for the rest of the trip.

We stay in a villa on the edge of town, again the only tenants. The villa has a shaded café that overlooks part of the oasis-fed vegetable and fruit fields and provides a fine view of the sunset over the desert.

The next day, we go into the desert to visit a long-abandoned *ksour,* one of the tenth-century castles typically built on hilltops to guard the trade routes and provide shelter for the traders. Until early in the twentieth century, Timimoun was the largest slave-trading center in North Africa. From there, we gaze out at the endless encroaching dunes of the Grand Erg Occidental.

Our driver heads into the dunes with his 4x4 and shows off his hair-raising driving skills until he gets stuck at the crest of a dune. With all of us helping to dig and push, we get unstuck. I hope this tempers his enthusiasm for such stunts. Environmental damage aside, there should be some places where vehicles cannot go and that remain the exclusive realm of hiker and camel.

Adrar

In contrast to the historical Timimoun, Adrar is a modern industrial city built by the government during the past decade, where piping for the natural gas pipeline is manufactured. It is a neatly laid-out town of forty-five thousand with fairly attractive red and yellow residential developments, schools, and public buildings. There is an enormous palm tree–lined central square with a towering monument for the martyrs.

Sidi N takes us on a tour of an old, nearly vacant casbah and an abandoned Jewish quarter. "In the past ten years," he says, "there have only been two tourists in Adrar. You. There is nothing here. Why did you put this place on your itinerary?"

In fact, this was the only destination included by the travel agency that we didn't handpick. We figured they knew what they were doing. "Wrong," says Sidi N. But we make the best of it, walking around the neighborhoods and just kicking back. The high point of the stay is dinner at an open-air grill, sitting on tree-trunk stools and watching the sweating chef carve up legs of lamb with a scimitar-sized knife that he flourishes theatrically. All the workers in the grill are from Mali. This triggers our curiosity about that country, which ultimately leads to our journey to Mali in 2012. We later find out from our travel agent that there are no daily flights from the Timmimoun area to Algiers and that the reason we were to stay overnight in Adrar was to wait for the next flight. Who knows? Perhaps we would not have gone to Mali had we not eaten at the grill in Adrar.

Algiers Redux and the Roman Ruins

Most of the day is spent in transit, but by late afternoon we are back in the Hotel Safir in Algiers. We have a corner room with windows on one side and French doors opening on a balcony that overlooks the harbor.

We unpack and relax for a while, then go for a walk before dinner. Many people are on the street downtown, strolling, window-shopping, hanging out. Suddenly, a young man comes from behind, grabs one of Barbara's gold earrings, and runs off, dodging pedestrians on the sidewalk. Fortunately, the earring comes off easily and her ear isn't injured, but she cries out, trips, and falls. I quickly determine that she's okay but mistakenly think he had grabbed her purse, so I give chase, shouting "Stop, thief!" My plea in English is in the wrong language. No one stops the thief or even tries (I should have shouted in French, "Au voleur!"). He ducks down a dark side street and I lose him. I'm not sure what I would have done had I caught him.

Barbara is shaken up but otherwise all right. She blames herself for wearing gold earrings, and we learn a valuable lesson: we no longer travel with personal items that we can't afford to lose.

Dinner with a half bottle of Coteaux de Mascara helps out. The incident is a sad blot on our Algerian experience, but it could have happened anywhere, including Brooklyn.

Cherchell and Tipasa are lovely seaside towns a couple of hours' drive west of Algiers. Cherchell is a bustling Mediterranean fishing port that happens to be sitting on vast Phoenician, Roman, and Byzantine ruins 2,000 to 2,500 years old. The city was called Caesarea by Juba II in the first century AD, at the height of its glory. On the way, we pull off the highway and drive up a high hill to see a tomb that, allegedly, was the burial place of Numidian royalty beginning in 500 BC. It may or may not contain the remains of Juba II and Cleopatra Selene, Juba's Queen and the daughter of Marc Antony and Cleopatra of Egypt. It seems that while his father, Juba I, spent his life and died fighting Roman domination of Algeria, Juba II served the Romans dutifully and well, administering Algeria to their great profit.

The tomb is a round pile of rock about thirty meters high and twice that in diameter. There is an entranceway, which is barred. According to Sidi N, there is nothing inside anyway, just one passageway that circles the perimeter and ends in an empty internment space. Because of its size and hilltop location, the tomb can be seen from many kilometers away. That's unfortunate because it is not particularly attractive. *Sic transit gloria mundi.*

In Cherchell, there seems to be ambivalence among the citizenry about the antiquities in their midst. They maintain a museum containing some particularly fine Roman sculptures. On the other hand, several sites in the city, including a substantial amphitheater and bath complex, are fenced off and littered with trash. While we sit in a crowded café (all male clientele except for Barbara), Sidi N informs us that discoveries of antiquities in the city are considered a nuisance by some, hindering commercial development. At the city center, there is a spacious and well-tended town square where children play in a two-thousand-year-old fountain while their mothers sit on segments of fluted columns. Sunburned old men in worn black suits use Corinthian capitals as tables for their espresso. The Cherchellians utilize the antiquities without revering them.

Tipaza, on the other hand, is quiet and small. The ruins are outside the town and extensive, spilling down dramatically to the sea. While Tipaza also offers lovely beaches and turquoise waters for weekenders from Algiers, the antiquities are very important to the local community, more than just for their economic impact. They are taken seriously and well maintained.

This Roman outpost was home to twenty thousand people in the fourth century AD. It had the typical Roman city grid layout, with a paved *decumanus* (main street connecting with the Roman coastal road) and *cardo maximus* (main cross street). Lining these streets are nearly intact amphitheaters, fountains, temples, granaries, barracks, stables, baths, and villas of the illuminati. Common folk, small traders, craftspersons, farmers, and herders lived on the side streets. Plazas and gardens abound, in which ancient olive trees still stand, providing shade, fruit, and beauty. The columned forum, or marketplace, lines both sides of the cardo maximus, as do more sumptuous villas, all with a stupendous view of the sea. The offshore breeze tempers the heat. One could spend days roaming the woods and cliffs of this beautiful site, imagining the well-ordered, luxurious life lived here by the Roman inhabitants. At least until the Vandals arrived in AD 372.

The next day, Sidi N shows up with his eighteen-year-old grandson as an alternate driver, and we make the trip to Djémila, originally called Cuicul during the Roman and Byzantine occupation in the first six centuries AD. It lies in the Kabiye Mountains in Northeastern Algeria, a region that has regularly produced revolutionaries, including those who fought the French, Berber tribes demanding more autonomy, and Islamic militants seeking national power.

Djémila (*the beautiful* in Arabic) was a Roman military outpost uncharacteristically constructed inland rather than on the coast. It is situated in an easily defensible position on a high ridge formed by the confluence of two rivers. The only aesthetic anomaly is that the triangular shape of the ridge did not easily accommodate the Roman preference for square grid urban design. As it grew to its peak population of twelve thousand, it spread from the point of the triangle uphill in successive waves of construction, known as the first city, second city, and third city. What was good for military defense in ancient times translates now into a spectacular view of the surrounding mountains and valleys.

We walk downhill from the entrance toward the third city, stunned by the extent and integrity of the ruins, which are more concentrated than those of Tipaza. There are few gardens and fewer,

Roman Theater, Djémila

but larger, fora and market areas. The efficiency and ingenuity of the water supply, waste disposal, traffic control, security measures, commercial facilities, and residential accommodations are remarkable. There is a fourteen-seat unisex stone privy that no doubt was the scene of some hilarity. A stone pedestal in front of one of the smaller buildings on the *cardo* bears the relief image of a large phallus and testicles. This may have been a simple fertility symbol, a sign for a brothel, or just boasting by the resident. Large structures, like the amphitheater and the Christian Basilica, sit outside the city's walls. We wander the grounds for hours, almost all alone, not a foreign tourist in sight.

Next, we visit a museum where statuary and mosaics from the ruins are restored and protected. The mosaics from the Roman and Byzantine villas are huge. Roman, Greek, and Phoenician mythological scenes, some blatantly erotic, join lives of the saints and depictions of hunting, farming, and bucolic bliss. The mosaics take up the walls and floors of the spacious museum.

We move on to Setif—birthplace of the final struggle for independence from France. During World War II, Algerians were encouraged by de Gaulle and other French politicians to join the Free French armies and fight for the Allies in Europe, with the promise that this would lead to independence. A parade to celebrate the Allies' victory in Europe was held in Setif on May 8, 1945. Relying on the French promise, the independence activists marched under their own banner. French troops and colonial militia fired upon them and chased them through the town, killing about one hundred activists. This led to reprisals against the colonists. The French army and air force responded with an all-out assault on the local population, killing an estimated forty thousand Algerians and marking the beginning of the end of French colonization in Algeria. The independence movement was largely nonviolent until November 1954, when the FLN formally turned to armed revolution, leading to independence in 1962.

I keep these things in mind when I walk through this modern bustling city, with its smart shoppers in western dress and its French-style, tree-lined boulevards superimposed on its few but well-tended ancient baths, fountains, and columnar fragments. It is hard to believe that this was once a war zone. The only conflict we witness in Setif is between Sidi N and a young guide at the Museum of Natural History, who argue over details of Algerian history and art, competing for our attention.

The drive back to Algiers is interminable. There are control roadblocks every few kilometers. Traffic is backed up as far as one can see. Progress is so slow that a young boy sits on the concrete slab of the highway meridian, selling paper cups of tea to the nearly stationary drivers. Between control points, Sidi's grandson drives like a madman. He gauges his progress by his proximity to a pickup truck heavily loaded with caged chickens. He dubs the pickup driver "Chicken Man," and we make a game of trying to stay ahead of him. We are relieved when Chicken Man finally turns off at an exit.

The next day, Sidi N drives us to the airport and speeds us through check-in and security. He is not wearing his khaki bill cap, so, in addition to a healthy tip, I give him my own khaki bill cap, which reads "Brooklyn Botanical Gardens." Smiling, he claps it on his head.

Ma salaama and *au revoir*, Algeria.

Epilogue

We have great respect for the Algerian people for their fierce resistance to colonialism, their tenacious struggle for independence, and their preservation of the unique and disparate cultures in the country.

But the issues that led to the civil war have not been resolved. Incidents of violence in 2007 led to predictions of an imminent slide back into the horrors of widespread armed conflict. It hasn't happened. Perhaps the extreme violence of the recent past has cauterized the societal wounds no one wants to open again.

We want to return. We want to see the Louvre of rock art in Djanel; to visit Oran, Tlemcen, and western Algeria; to walk among the Roman ruins at Timgud; and to spend more time in the Kabyle Mountains with Sidi of the North and other Algerians, even vagabonds.

Nepal:

Nepal. The name evokes images of Edmund Hillary and Tenzing Norgay waving their nations' flags at the top of the world; of climbers, Sherpas, and porters crossing the shifting crevices of the Khumbu Ice Fall, balancing on aluminum ladders; of multicolor prayer pennants snapping in gale force winds in the Annapurna base camp; of the colossal spindrift of snow that the global jet stream blows off the top of Mount Everest; of earthquakes, avalanches, and sudden fierce storms.

Nepal is a climber's and trekker's Nirvana. It has the most spectacular mountain scenery on the planet. Its borders encompass eight of the world's ten highest peaks, whose ascents have been the subjects of countless books, films, and legends. And I thought that books, films, and legends were as close as I would ever get to Nepal.

The California Sierras, Colorado Rockies, and White Mountains of New Hampshire were challenging enough for me. But during a Sierra Club backpack outing in 2004, Barbara and I get to know Melinda Goodwater, coleader of the trip, who is married to Singaman Lama, a Nepali and tour organizer in Kathmandu. Melinda spends half the year leading Sierra Club outings in the US and the other half in Nepal guiding tours with Singa. In Nepal, she and Singa prefer to avoid the popular Everest Base Camp Trek or the Annapurna Circuit, which are crowded with too many tourists who leave their junk behind. Instead, they find alternate routes that are beautiful and far less traveled.

In the summer of 2010, when Barbara and I discuss where to travel next, we remember Melinda's descriptions of Nepal. We make contact via email and discuss our Nepal options; she is aware of our strengths and limitations and believes we can handle an extended Himalayan trek. So Nepal it is, in November of 2010.

We have other reasons to choose Nepal. Barbara's twenty-year-old niece, Rachel, is studying in Kathmandu and living with a Nepali family. We would like to see her and have her show us around the sprawling city. Finally, we could take a few days after the mountain trek to visit a place we had never heard of: Chitwan National Park in southern Nepal.

Exhausted and jet-lagged after twenty-five hours in transit, we land at the Kathmandu International Airport in the late afternoon on November 6. Melinda picks us up and takes us to the Potala Guest House, where we meet our fellow trekkers, Gordon Duvaul and Suzanne Swedo, both of whom are in our age group and have trekked in Nepal before. We already know Suzanne; she was the other leader of the 2004 Sierra Club trip. Suzanne has written books about hiking, camping, and wildflowers. Gordon wants to run a marathon in every state of the Union and has only a few left to reach his goal.

Gordon's and Suzanne's hiking backgrounds are intimidating. However, we are in pretty good shape ourselves. I am seventy-two, but I swam competitively in a Masters program for fifteen years and completed six triathlons in my sixties. Barbara, sixty-six, is a distance runner. And for the trek, porters will carry the heavy stuff—tents, cooking gear, food, etc.—while we carry daypacks with necessities and a change of clothes. We are nervous but excited.

Nepal is one of the poorest countries in the world, and Kathmandu, its capital and largest city, reflects that. The Potala Guest House is on the border of what is called the Old Town, the center of the city. There are charming centuries-old buildings, shrines and temples, and narrow winding streets and alleys to get pleasantly lost in. With few exceptions, these structures are in poor condition, in need of repair and repainting. Power outages occur daily. Beggars are everywhere. Fortunately, for some in the travel business, so are tourists.

We spend our first morning in Nepal meeting some of the Sherpas and porters who will accompany us for the next two weeks. Sherpas are an ethnic group that, long ago, migrated from Tibet to the Nepali highlands. They live on a subsistence economy, supplemented by their earnings as guides, cooks, and porters. They are strong, tireless, sure-footed, and invariably cheerful, and their first concern is the safety of the client. Most of the Sherpas on our trek are from the same village in the Langtang Valley and have worked with Melinda and Singa before.

In the afternoon, Rachel gives us a tour of Kathmandu—Durbar Square, with its temples and palaces in sad disrepair, and the Ghat, where bodies are being cremated along the river. That she is fluent in the language surprises and delights the natives; she looks nothing like them. In stark contrast to the Nepalis, who are dark-haired and short of stature, she is blonde and nearly six feet tall. Her language skills and her height make her a worthy guide.

The Trek

The trek is known as the Langtang and Gosainkunda Lake Trek. The first part is a five-day round trip starting and ending near the town of Syabrubesi (altitude, 4,820 feet). The route follows the Langtang

River Valley upstream to Langshisha Kharka lake (altitude, 13,450 feet). The second part is an eleven-day trek that follows the Langtang River Valley downstream, visits the holy Gosainkunda lakes, goes over the Laurebina La pass (altitude, 15,120 feet), and descends to the Kathmandu Valley.

We begin by carrying our gear through the crowded streets of Kathmandu to meet a chartered bus that will take us to the trail-head near Syabrubesi. We wait on a street corner until an old bus, full of Nepalis (at least eighteen), with piles of gear tied on its roof, pulls up. "This is it," Singa says, and he starts tossing our duffels onto the roof. We jam into bus seats meant for smaller people, and the bus takes off. Jerry cans of kerosene block the aisle. A young man is playing the tabla; others are joking with the driver. The scenery consists of rocks, more rocks, patches of cultivation, and the occasional glimpse of snow-covered peaks. The bus is slow, grinding its way up the foothills.

When the bus gets into the real mountains, the road narrows to one lane, skirting hairpin turns and sheer drops. The driver rarely shifts out of first or reverse gear. I'm scared stiff, but after a while I decide to trust the driver, relax, and enjoy the ride. The trip, which only covers about twenty-two miles, takes eight hours.

At four p.m., we arrive at Syabrubesi and rush to unload our gear in a field before dark. The porters set up tents, and the cook fixes a great vegetarian dinner—soup, pepper bread, dal, rice, mushrooms, and potatoes.

The next morning, we are up and out at seven thirty a.m. Getting to our next destination requires a net elevation gain of more than three thousand feet. We pass old and quaint stone bridges, playful langur monkeys, gurgling waterfalls—or so we are told. Instead, we spend most of the time staring straight ahead at the trail and sitting down whenever the lead (Melinda or Singa) stops. The altitude has finally gotten to us New York City flatlanders. Fortunately, it hits us not in the form of throbbing headaches or nausea—just fatigue. We're used to more oxygen—or whatever it is we breathe in Brooklyn. It is a one-foot-in-front-of-the-other slog, but the legs hold up and we make it to a group of lodges called Lama Hotel.

We set up tents in a pasture adjoining the lodges after the porters shovel yak dung out of the way. It's very cold in the tent. Drinking pots of tea results in many trips outside to relieve ourselves during the night. A nearby dog decides to bark for an hour and a half. We wear everything we have but still can't get warm. Our flashlight quits. Meanwhile, the porters, Sherpas, and the cook are singing and playing cards in a tent a few feet away. Yaks come and go, snuffling and defecating. We laugh, huddle together, and, eventually, sleep.

The next morning, we climb another three thousand feet from Lama Hotel to the village of Langtang (altitude, 11,250 feet), a popular stopover for trekkers, hikers, and climbers. The village is built on the flat bottom of the Valley, with the glacier-draped, twenty-thousand-foot mountains Langtang Lirung and Langtang II looming over it. There are about two hundred permanent

Langtang Village, with our tents in the foreground

residents, with capacity for dozens of visitors. The buildings are one or two stories high, with corrugated steel roofs. Villagers tend gardens of potatoes and greens. Yaks roam free in adjacent pastures, and horses are herded through the broad unpaved streets.

Along the way, Barbara takes hundreds of photos, many of the stupendous surrounding landscape but many more of the strong, tough, smiling, and gentle Nepali. Throughout the trek, she is concerned that exposure to the cold will drain her camera battery. A clerk at a camera store in New York had advised her to sleep with the camera close to her heart; I can attest that she followed his advice.

Gradually acclimating to the altitude, we struggle with the other difficulties of the trail. Feeder streams, tributaries of the Langtang River, have carved deep gullies and canyons in their passage from the mountain glaciers to the river. When the trail crosses these streams, we must negotiate steep, often wet, descents and ascents. The descents are the worst. A slip on the way down can send us tobogganing on our backsides for many feet before we are brought

River crossing

up sharply and painfully by a protruding rock, errant root, or hapless comrade. On steep descents, we think about where and how to place our feet, weight, and poles for every step. Despite the greater exertion required for going up, we regard ascents as a relief from the tension generated by going down.

There is, of course, the crossing of a stream itself. It is the dry season in Nepal, so stepping-stones are visible due to the low water levels. Were we nimble, like the Sherpas, we could hop from rock to rock to the other side. Instead, we proceed deliberately in stately consideration of each step, using poles dug into the streambed for balance. Some of the streams have cut canyons so deep, rough, and steep that suspension bridges have been built for the crossing. These are steel mesh affairs, about five feet wide and one hundred or so feet long. There is a waist-high cable on each side to hang onto, but the bridge twists and sways as I shift my weight with each step. I can see the awful drop through the mesh floor and hear the churning rapids of the stream below. I focus ten feet ahead on a metal strip that runs down the center of the bridge, hang on to both cables, repeat to myself, *don't look down*, and hope a yak doesn't come the other way.

Every few kilometers, we see an isolated settlement with a teahouse and one or two other structures. As in Langtang village, all of the buildings are roofed with sheets of corrugated steel, manufactured in 65-kilogram (143-pound) segments. Since yaks are unable to carry these loads of steel on the rough, steep, twisting trails, the remaining option is human transport. Two or three times a day, a warning that porters are approaching is passed down the line of trekkers. We step off the trail to give them room, and within minutes they appear, bent over, wearing worn sneakers, each with a steel roofing segment on his back, leaping from rock to rock. This is a feat of strength and balance, and also an example of the extreme hardships the Sherpa people must endure in order to make a living. Our existential musings on why we trek at our age seem petty compared to the transport porter's certain knowledge of why he does what he does.

We develop a day-to-day rhythm, doing the same arduous climbing and descending, inching our way up and down the tall, smooth, slippery stones, and taking long strides on the level stretches. We engage in extended conversation with a comrade or hike alone in quiet contemplation. Barbara learns a lot from Suzanne about the flora of the region, and Suzanne learns a lot from Barbara about treatment for aching knees. It feels good to challenge our physical limits, but we look forward to stopping for rest breaks, lunches, and dinners. There is some danger in what we're doing—avalanches, landslides, earthquakes, freezing, and, mainly, falling. These are the risks we accept in order to trespass on these stony peaks and take in their fearsome beauty. It's a risk we can minimize if we are focused, strong, and determined. The rest is up to nature, which doesn't care.

Holy man, Lake Gosainkunda, Nepal

Lake Gosainkunda

The scenery is overwhelming, especially in the early morning and late afternoon, when the slanted rays of the sun set the permanent snow caps of the surrounding peaks on fire. We see a similar effect, on a fraction of the scale, from our apartment in Brooklyn as the evening sun lights up Manhattan's metal-clad towers. On relatively level stretches, we are able to look up from the trail to appreciate the views around us: rhododendron forests and glaciers; alpine pastures dotted with shaggy black-coated yaks; villages high on knife-edge ridge tops or spread on the flat floor of the valley; tiny teahouses built of stone and timber; morning seas of fog filling the valley until burned off by the rising sun; and Buddhist shrines and temples adorned with banners and pennants of gold, silver, crimson, azure, and green. What we don't see many of are other trekkers.

We spend two nights at the Gosainkunda lakes, the highest encampment of our lives (altitude, 14,430 feet). The lakes are shallow glacial ponds studded with cairns, tiny towers of stacked rocks. These lakes, sacred to both Buddhists and Hindus, are the destination of thousands of holy men who make a pilgrimage every August to leave more stone towers.

A shallow open dugout near the shore of the most sacred lake is home to a holy man. The dugout is walled with rocks and the floor covered with sandy gravel. He is naked except for a bright-orange loincloth and arm bracelets. His skin is nut brown, his hair long and matted. He is thin and sinewy, with well-defined ribs and muscles. According to Singa, he is a permanent resident here. We share our food with him.

All our meals on the trail are served alfresco. A large decorative carpet is spread out, and we sit on it with the porters and Sherpas, shivering in the dark, hugging mugs of tea. Once again, we regret that, in our effort to pack light, we had not brought enough warm clothes. The cook brings out the food, starting with a big, delicious steaming pot of soup that warms the body and calms the mind. Plates of rice, lentils, beans, pepper bread, noodles, vegetables—and occasionally mutton, chicken, or goat—follow.

Our dessert is a blanket of stars, circumscribed by the jagged black silhouette of the Langtang Range.

On November 23, our fourteenth day on the trail, we are to descend from our camp at Magungap (11,440 feet) to Khukmanung (8,035 feet).

It is raining. There is the usual up-and-down stream crossing, but mostly the trail is downhill and dangerous, on steep, rain-slicked rocks. We go at it for two or three hours. Melinda, Singa, and Gordon are two hundred yards ahead, and Barbara is fifteen to twenty yards behind me. Suddenly, I hear her cry out. I scramble back up the trail to find her sitting on the ground rocking back and forth, holding her right arm and moaning in pain. A Sherpa is holding her. Her foot and pole had slipped, and she had fallen on her elbow. Barbara is shivering and pale and about to go into shock. She tries to stand and walk but passes out for a few seconds. We put our jackets around her. A Sherpa bounds down the trail to get Melinda and Singa, while another Sherpa appears with a first aid kit and wraps the arm to immobilize it and stop the swelling.

Barbara is in a great deal of pain, shaking her head. Her right arm looks twisted and mangled—she is sure it's broken. I feel helpless. All I can do is hold her. Melinda and Singa come up the trail, confer, and make a decision: Barbara will be carried down to the nearby village of Khutumsang where they can call for a helicopter to take her to a hospital in Kathmandu.

The Sherpas, porters, and local villagers quickly fashion a basket into a seat. A villager uses a foot-and-a-half-long *kukri* knife to cut down and strip a sapling for a backrest. They lift her into the seat and carry her on their backs, alternating carriers every hundred yards and making the transfers so gently that Barbara is only dimly aware of what is happening. Fortunately, she is thin, weighing only about 105 pounds. It takes about thirty minutes to reach the village.

Melinda calls for a helicopter, but it's engaged. Barbara lapses in and out of consciousness. After two hours, the chopper appears, and we fly off for a twenty-minute ride over the Kathmandu Valley to the Kathmandu Airport. In the seat of my very first helicopter ride, the bird's-eye perspective is startling, but under the circumstances not particularly enjoyable for either of us. A van is waiting to take us to the CIWEC, a British-funded clinic specializing in orthopedic injuries.

To everyone's great relief, preliminary views from the x-rays show a complete dislocation but no fracture. The orthopedic surgeon, Deepak Masala, confirms the x-ray reading. He is a short, dapper Nepali with an open and positive manner, inspiring confidence. He and the entire staff speak fluent English.

Dr. Masala proposes that he attempt a closed reduction (pulling or pushing the bone back into its joint without surgery) at the clinic under partial sedation. The other option would require going to an operating hospital for surgery under general anesthesia. Barbara and I readily agree to his first recommendation. Dr. Masala has seen many elbow fractures, but this is only the second dislocation he has treated in his fifteen years of practice. He asks whether I want to stay in the room while he pulls on Barbara's arm to pop the elbow back into place. I quickly decline. I'm concerned that my reaction may result in his having another patient to treat.

Barbara later tells me that Dr. Masala and his assistant pulled on the arm twice, causing much pain but failing to reduce the dislocation. They need an additional puller. The doctor comes into the waiting room to request my help again, and I decline for a second time, knowing I would be hesitant to cause more pain, probably botching the attempt in the process. Dr. Masala then turns to a nearby security guard, who is bigger and stronger than I am. He agrees. Barbara reports that they took up their positions like a tug-of-war team, pulled, and the elbow snapped back into its socket on the first try, stopping the severe pain immediately.

We stay at the clinic until ten p.m., waiting for x-rays to confirm that the reduction is firmly set. Barbara is given a cast and sling. The bill for the entire treatment and the staff's first-rate services, including x-rays, closed reduction, medication, and a follow-up visit, totals nine hundred dollars. We're amazed. At least one extra zero would have been added to the cost if the accident had occurred in New York City. The only drawback, a small one, is having to wait for the traveling "cashier" to appear with his somewhat outdated credit card reader. Apparently, "have reader, will travel" is a profitable enterprise in Kathmandu. Once Barbara is discharged, we round out the day's excitement with a very late dinner at a Nepalese restaurant.

The next two days, we wander through some of the usual tourist stops—Badoe Square in Patan, with its beautifully maintained Palace Museum, and Boktipur, where we buy an antique mandala.

The Nepali family Rachel is staying with invites us for dinner. Melinda tells us that it's appropriate for guests to bring fruit, so we arrive with a bag of oranges. The family lives in a two-story house in a newer part of Kathmandu. The father is a civil servant and the mother a teacher. They love Rachel, who has established a close friendship with their own daughter, Safal, also a student.

The dinner is vegetarian and delicious. Nepalis eat with their hands, but the family has thoughtfully put forks next to our plates. I attempt to eat, albeit clumsily, with my fingers. Barbara, however, has a problem. Using the left hand to eat is regarded as unclean, and her right arm is now in a sling. She apologizes profusely and compromises by using her left hand and the fork. I have no excuse and sit on my left hand to keep myself from using it.

Over dinner, we talk politics. A Maoist movement, active in the countryside for many years, reached a truce with the bourgeoisie two years ago to form a coalition government, but they have not yet agreed on a constitution. Another dinner topic is the caste system, which plays a big role in Nepali society. Safal's parents would never allow their daughter to marry a *dalit*, a lower-caste peasant. She would be shunned if she did.

Sherpas, Sing Gompa

On the last official day of the trek, everybody gets together at the Yak, a big, noisy Nepali restaurant. Sherpas, porters, tour leaders, trekkers, and the cook are all present at one long table. They drink prodigious amounts of Everest Beer. There is a special round of applause for the cook, who consistently turned out delicious, comforting, and nutritious meals under demanding conditions. He seldom goes home to his village during trekking season and is staying in the city until his next trek. For him, getting home involves a twenty-two-hour bus ride and three days' walk.

The food comes to the table—smoking platters of tandoori chicken, lentils, green beans, and roasted potatoes. There is raucous feasting, drinking, and laughing. Fulsome tips are distributed, and many embraces are exchanged. We express special thanks to the sixty-four-year-old Sherpa who carried Barbara most of the way down the mountain after she fell.

It's very sad to say good-bye to the Sherpas. I think about our different destinations. We will fly home to our comfortable apartment in Brooklyn and our life of writing, photography, travel, and indulgence in New York's cultural offerings. The Sherpas return to their difficult, dangerous, and poorly paid trade (their livelihood dependent on the availability of willing tourists), the arbitrary preferences of tour agencies, and the formidable vagaries of Himalayan weather.

Chitwan

Barbara's arm feels well enough for us to finish our tour of Nepal at the Chitwan National Park. The bus ride from Kathmandu to Chitwan takes six hours, and we're the only tourists on board. Halfway through, the driver stops the bus and invites the passengers to relieve themselves. The women go to one side of the road and the men to the other. Since the ground slopes down from the road, with the bus between both sides, there is some measure of privacy. No one, Barbara included, is fazed by this arrangement.

The national park is in the southeast of Nepal in an area known as the Terai—the plains. The climate is much different from that of the Himalayas—hot and, except for the dry season, wet. The Park has almost one hundred square miles of wetland, grassland, and forest. Within its borders dwell spotted deer, sambol deer, gharielles, macaques, crocodiles, sloth bears, eagles, civet cats, Bengal tigers, rhinos, and wild elephants.

Our hotel is located just outside the park boundaries. We take an elephant ride, which is not your ordinary circus oval track stroll. The elephant dives into the forest like a lifeboat into the sea, crunching through head-high underbrush and tearing off overhanging branches with its trunk. Curious to learn more of the lives of the elephants, we visit an elephant training center and are appalled by what we see—young tuskers are taken from their mothers at five years of age, and adult elephants are disciplined by chaining two of their legs to pillars. This treatment leads to pathological nervous behavior. Elephants should be left in the wild, matriarchs of entire herds, stomping on hunters who come for their babies or their ivory.

We ask to take a jungle walk, hoping to see animals in their natural habitat. I assume that the guides are not going to expose tourists on foot to the dangerous and predatory animals roaming the park and that, therefore, we will stay close to the hotel. I expect to see nothing more threatening than birds, monkeys, and deer. Not so. Our naturalist guide, Komar, gives a short lecture on what to do if confronted by sloth bears, tigers, rhinos, and elephants. We take off on a trail straight into the forest. Komar and a local Thoru tribe villager lead the way, armed with bamboo walking sticks. I drop back and pick up a heavy branch that I know would be useless against most of these animals but that makes me feel better.

During this dry season, the foliage is thinned out, and the midday sun shines through the trees. We see sambol and spotted deer and macaques, but little else. I relax. About one hour into the forest, the Thoru villager tells us to stop and remain quiet and motionless. Komar says they have spotted a mother rhino with two babies standing in a mud hole. We peer through the dry bushes and, sure enough, there they are, about fifty feet away, turned broadside to us, apparently unaware of our presence. Barbara wants a picture, but Komar vetoes that. "If the mother spots us," he says, "She'll charge." He borrows Barbara's camera, says he'll sneak up closer to get a picture, and disappears.

Rhinos! What did they say about charging rhinos? Run in a zigzag pattern or climb a tree. But rhinos can go twenty-five miles per hour straight through brush. In my prime and on an unobstructed track, I might have been able to sprint at about half that pace—but I'm no longer in my prime. A tree is a better option. But how is Barbara going to climb a tree with one arm in a cast and sling? Quickly, I look around for a tree that I can push her up into and maybe follow behind. While I'm so engaged, Barbara sees the mother rhino turn her head slowly toward us. Suddenly, Komar reappears and says, "She's facing us now, and I think she's ready to charge. Now is the time to run. She won't go far from her babies."

We run. Fortunately, the rhino does not.

The next day, we head back to Kathmandu and fly home on December 1, 2010, with stories to tell.

Epilogue

On April 18, 2014, an ice avalanche on Mount Everest kills sixteen Sherpas, making it the worst climbing disaster on the mountain up until that time. Grief-stricken and angry at what they rightly perceive as unfair treatment by tour agencies and the government, the Sherpas petition the Ministry of Tourism for better pay, working conditions, and insurance, as well as the construction of a memorial to the dead. The government's response is woefully inadequate. The

Sherpas refuse to work for the rest of the season in honor of their fallen comrades.

Almost exactly one year later, on April 25, 2015, avalanches, rockslides, and pressure waves triggered by earthquakes completely level Langtang Village and several other villages in the Langtang Valley. Hundreds are dead or missing. There are few survivors. In news photos, the valley where Langtang Village once stood looks like someone scraped it clean. I think of the people we saw during our stay in Langtang and our Sherpas, who were from a nearby community that had also suffered heavy damage. Melinda Goodwater and Singaman Lama are raising funds for the rebuilding of these villages and relief for the survivors.

On August 15, 2016, tragedy strikes again. An overloaded bus with seventy-five passengers, some clinging to the roof, veers off a narrow mountain road and plunges nearly one thousand feet, rolling over and over. Thirty-three passengers are killed, and many are severely injured. The driver is found unconscious in a tree.

The bitter irony is that most of the passengers of the ill-fated bus were returning to their home villages to collect government cash certificates as compensation for the loss of family members and damages suffered in the earthquakes and avalanches of 2015.

Cameroon:

SONGS OF THE BAKA

We stay close together as we follow the local guide through the Dja Forest Reserve deep in the eastern Cameroon rain forest. Most of the time I cannot make out a trail. The red clay forest floor is covered with leaves and an undergrowth of vines that trip us and stickers that catch at our clothes. Visibility is about twenty feet. The guide often stops to clear the trail with his machete. While we wait, tiny black ants crawl up our legs and respond to our idle scratches by biting and holding on. We continue, pulling the ants off and cursing.

Barbara is behind me, followed by our Cameroon guide, Jonas "Jones" Nijfuouta; a Forest Ranger (mandatory within the Reserve); and two Bantu porters carrying twenty-five-pound bags of rice and salt and our tents. We are seeking the encampment of a band of Baka Pygmy.

We spent the previous night at Mama Rose's hostel in the Bantu village of Somalomo on the edge of the Reserve. In the morning, the porters paddled us upstream on the Dja River in a leaky pirogue, fighting the twisting currents that ran deep under the Dja's deceptively calm black surface. Jones is a big and amiable man. It is the first and only time we have seen him afraid. He confesses that he cannot swim. Not until the porters beach the boat does he relax.

The trek into the rain forest is the culmination of a twenty-one-day visit to Cameroon. Our goal is to meet, observe, and interact with people whose way of life is largely, if not completely, unaffected by contemporary Western culture and technology. We chose Cameroon because it has a wide variety of such traditional cultures.

Just as I become resigned to a long, indefinite slog, we hear voices and smell wood smoke. The guide gives a brief shout, eliciting laughter. After a few more turns in the trail, we stop, stunned to behold a scene that our distant forbears might have encountered.

Before us is a gently sloping half-acre of land cleared of underbrush. Several ironwood trees stand in the clearing like Roman columns, their arches, one hundred feet high, forming the forest canopy. Fifteen huts made of sprung sapling frames thatched with dried leaves are scattered about the clearing. Clouds of fragrant smoke rise from smoldering logs in front of each hut, the smoke hanging above the camp like burnt incense in a temple. At the base of the slope, just inside the entrance to the camp, is a hard-packed area, about twenty feet square, bordered by crude tree-branch benches.

It takes a while before we notice two men in grass skirts sprawled on one of the benches. They return our greeting with a nod and a smile but remain seated and are otherwise impassive. Jones encourages us to walk around the compound. As we do, other Baka, mostly women and small children, emerge from their huts. When not attending to the infants, the women are busy at various tasks: chopping manioc, a starchy derivative of the cassava root, making grass skirts, and sorting ground nuts. The children play in the dirt, staring at us and staying close to the women. A gray-haired man squats in front of a smoking fire, curing green tobacco leaves.

"Where are all the other men?" we ask. The women tell us that most are out hunting and trapping and will return by evening. A few,

Baka boy at home

Roasting tobacco

who had hunted the day before, rest in the camp. Some women are gathering wild food.

Our conversations are slow and halting. The local guide translates their answers to Jones in French, who then converts the responses to English. The process reverses when we ask a question. But the system appears to work because everyone is smiling patiently.

The Baka are not unlike the Pygmies I recall pictured in National Geographic magazines. The adults stand about four and a half feet tall. However, the Pygmies in those magazines invariably looked sullen, bony-limbed, and poorly nourished, with protruding bellies, some wearing cast-off western clothing. The Baka in this encampment are solidly built and good-humored. Their legs are short and muscular, their arms long and slender. The men are barrel-chested. The women are full-bodied and proud of it. No one is obese. Baka noses are flat, their skin French Roast brown. They are tough and strong, able to carry loads of dressed game, fish, or baskets of wild root vegetables and fruit over miles of rough trails.

We look inside their huts. They sleep on pads made of sticks and leaves. Jones says that, if necessary, they can break down and transport an entire encampment in minutes.

The dress code here is grass skirt. The smallest children go naked or wear tiny green leaf skirts held up by woven twine. The one exception is an infant in a striped shirt who is wrapped in a red blanket. The women pass babies around, occasionally handing them off to be hugged and cuddled by the men.

There are several school-age children in the camp. According to Jones, Baka children don't go to school and cannot read. However, by adolescence they know every footpath and game trail in their region of the forest. They can climb almost any tree. They know what berries to pick, what plants are edible, what mushrooms are not, what herbs to cure which ailments. They know how to hunt, fish, trap, and live in the wild. And they know how to dance, drum, and sing.

Chief of the Baka

The chief and the men who have been hunting and trapping return by midafternoon. Most tumble into their huts for hard-earned rest. The chief, a robust man in his late forties, smiles at us and is very pleased when our porters present to him the sacks of rice and salt, food they otherwise must trade for.

I question the chief about the band's food sources. For the most part, he says, they live on "bush meat" plus fish; edible plants such as yams, taro root, and cassava; and wild fruit, mushrooms, bird eggs, and honey. Most of the meat comes from small animals caught in traps—mole rats, monkeys, and small antelope. They kill larger antelope with spears. They also spear "bush pigs." I envision these as little piglets, but they turn out to be dagger-tusked wild boar weighing up to three hundred pounds.

The chief volunteers that they don't have firearms and don't kill protected animals, like chimpanzees, lowland gorillas, or elephants. But for occasional trade of bush meat for grain with the Bantu, the Baka are among the world's last pure hunters and gatherers.

The Baka culture is one of the oldest on earth. They are semi-nomadic, moving their small camps when threatened by natural forces or outsiders, such as farmers, mining developers, logging companies, and hostile Bantu. They also leave when an area becomes overhunted—this band last moved when their camp was flooded.

Their religion is a simple belief in benevolent forest spirits who provide for them. Their economy is communal. They share the forest's provender and care for one another. They are peaceful. Yet Pygmies throughout Central Africa suffer discrimination and often violence at the hands of the majority Bantu-speaking Africans. The Pygmies are regarded as less than human, with malevolent supernatural powers that enable them to live in the fearful rain forest and that can be used against the Bantu. Pygmies have been hunted and killed like animals by belligerents in the civil war raging in the Democratic Republic of the Congo. Attempts to settle in Bantu villages often lead to unhappy results for the Pygmies, who are exploited and marginalized.

Just as twilight filters through the forest roof, Mama Rose and two porters arrive with trays of chicken, fish, and manioc. She assumes, correctly, that we might hesitate to share a Baka dinner of boiled mole rat. Mama Rose and her porters will sleep in the camp to avoid nocturnal encounters with leopards on their return trip.

Night falls quickly under the dark-green forest canopy, the only illumination the flickering red dots of a dozen small cooking fires scattered across the slope of the camp. We finish our meal and sit in the dark, waiting for the Baka to finish theirs.

Then, someone in the darkness takes a few warm-up riffs on a drum. Jones says the chief has deemed the arrival of the salt and rice a cause for celebration. About fifteen women, ranging in age from midteens to midsixties, and two young boys, about age seven or eight, all in grass skirts, shuffle into the square where we sit. Three drums begin a complicated rhythm, and the women begin to sing.

Baka singing is unique, featuring polyphonic and contrapuntal complexity combined with improvised lyrics. It is mesmerizing. The singers dance in a circle, but in the dark I can barely discern their movement. I chance switching on my headlamp, expecting a loud protest from the celebrants. But they give no notice to the light and continue without pause. They perform a quick, shuffling two-step while their hips shake double time. Now and then, a young woman initiates a call-and-answer sequence, interjecting an ad lib that evokes raucous laughter. The chief joins the circle for a few minutes, slowing the pace with a deliberate circling port-a-bras movement, then retires from the scene.

After an hour, the laughing dancers pause, sweat glistening on their bare torsos, and re-form into two lines facing each other on either side of the hard-packed floor of the square. The drumming and singing resumes. The dancers play a game where one darts across the square and tags an opposite member, who runs back with the original dancer to tag a person of her choice, and so on. Their dancing, singing, and gaming goes on without a break for over two hours.

The complex rhythms of the drums, the haunting harmonics of the singers, and the bodies of the tireless dancers shining in the smoky half-light come together to create an overwhelming, unforgettable sensory feast. Finally, exhausted, we stand up to leave. The Baka sing a song wishing us pleasant dreams. They would have danced all night had we so desired, our local guide tells us the next morning.

We sleep soundly in our tent, thankful for its rain fly, which deflects a midnight downpour. It's not called the rain forest for nothing. In the early morning, slipping and sliding in the red mud, we bid good-bye to the Baka, who smile and wave. Three women precede us down the path for about a hundred yards, singing a lovely cyclical, polyphonic song that wishes us a safe and happy journey. Their song is a perfect coda to an extraordinary experience.

Cameroon: Microcosm of Sub-Saharan Africa

Cameroon is a microcosm of the climatic and geographic diversity of sub-Saharan Africa. This diversity has led to the development of different cultures within Cameroon as people adapted to their particular surroundings. During our time there, we visit three geographic and cultural zones: the Southeast rain forest with its Baka Pygmy hunter-gatherers; the arid northern plateau with its pastoral nomads; and the fertile Southwest with its Bamileke agricultural kingdoms.

Aside from their grass skirts, the Baka forgo ornamentation. At the other end of the fashion spectrum, M'bororo and Dwayo women in northern Cameroon wear brightly colored clothes, beads, wire bracelets, anklets, and four or five watches with shiny metal bands on their arms. Whether or not the watches actually work is irrelevant. They also tattoo or scarify their faces, braid their hair, and shave their heads in elaborate designs.

Northern nomads decorate their utilitarian objects as well as their faces and bodies. The women create exquisite woven mats and etch calabash bowls with black geometric designs. Invited into a Dwayo hut, we see several mats and bowls. I make an offer for the mat with the most complex and interesting design. Demurring, the woman says, "It took a month to make that mat, and I have not finished looking at it." We choose another, pay her, and she adds, "This is the first money I have seen in months." Their transactions invariably involve cattle rather than coin.

Many other aspects of the lives, and even the deaths, of the members of the pastoral tribes revolve around cattle. When the cows run out of grass, the entire village picks up and moves to a better grazing area. Jones tells us that when a Dwayo is terminally ill and the community has to move to follow the herd, they leave him with shelter, food, and a cow. If he dies, whoever finds and buries him is

Baka woman

entitled to take the cow. The village will never again return to that site. If someone finds him and he recovers, the person who helped is given three cows. In that case, the tribe will return. A M'bororo woman tells us, "The most important things in our lives, are cattle, family, and clan—in that order."

Country does not make the short list. There are reasons for this. The European colonists drew national borders that had little to do with the traditional tribal areas. When the leaders of the anticolonial independence movement assumed power, they took care of their own family, clan, and tribe, handing out government positions, business opportunities, and other forms of largesse. They neglected the rest of the populace, especially those in remote villages. These isolated groups expect little from the government—and they're not disappointed.

Left alone, these tribes cling to traditional systems of justice, independent of the central government. In the far northern town of Poli, we are invited to attend the trial of a domestic civil case presided over by the local chief. Court, held every Tuesday between four and six in the afternoon, convenes in a clearing shaded by tall trees. Litigants, witnesses, and the public sit on blankets forming a semicircle facing the chief, who sits on an upright chair. We sit on a bench near the chief.

The case involves a love triangle. A young woman has taken her infant daughter and left her husband to be with a younger man she loves. The chief hears testimony from both sides. The woman, in a bright pink shirt, red skirt, and blue headscarf, tells the chief that she will not go back to her husband. The husband, looking grim, says that he would like his wife and child to return. The chief rules that the woman does not have to live with her husband, but that the young man must reimburse the husband for all the gifts the husband had brought to the woman's parents to gain their consent to the marriage. Unfortunately, the young man has nothing. He will be confined in the village until his parents bring the bovine or cash (unlikely) equivalent of the verdict. The court's business is done in an orderly manner, and there are no emotional displays. The husband and the paramour accept the verdict.

Much of the western highlands of Cameroon is divided into small hereditary kingdoms. We have the opportunity to stay for a few days with the king (or *Fon)* of one of them, a robust, intelligent forty-two-year-old man with a permanently furrowed brow. He and his four wives, nineteen children, countless grandchildren, brothers and sisters, uncles and aunts, and his father's widows live in the same compound. As the eldest son of the deceased chief, he is responsible for the support of all of them. His duties also include resolving property and domestic relations disputes in his entire village. He has also established a school at the edge of the compound for the village's children. Although he receives a stipend from the government for performing his royal duties, he is constantly driven by the needs of his extended family. For additional income, he has had to resort to providing accommodations for travelers such as us.

Over beers on his front porch, the king and I have several pleasant conversations about his duties, about the Grand Fon, who lives in a palace and to whom he reports, and about his garden, the dialogue animated by gestures in aid of his halting English and my halting French. Visibly proud, he shows me that his accommodations are listed in the Lonely Planet guidebook. In a large, dusty courtyard at the center of the compound, Barbara wanders around in the midafternoon heat, watching small children running and playing with makeshift toys and women attending to each other's hair, combing, braiding, and twisting.

Our farewell dinner is fresh vegetables from the king's extensive gardens and fish from the royal fish pond. Barbara and I insist on helping the four wives in the preparation of the meal. Under the critical supervision of Wife Number One, I chop vegetables until an enormous free-range white hen with a beak like a needle-nose plier pecks one of my toes. Unhappy with Barbara's chopping techniques and defensive about her hen, Wife Number One shoos us out of her courtyard kitchen.

There is vintage Scotch after the fine multicourse feast and traditional Bamileke music from a well-stocked stereo.

All in all, it's good to be king.

But only a few get to be king. The rest get by on little more than a subsistence-level economy. But they know how to party. We attend several celebrations for the millet harvest, and each involves dancing, chanting, and drumming—with the women leading the dances and the men on drums. Everyone is laughing, joking, drinking, and feasting as if they didn't have a worry in the world, when in fact there is always the specter of drought, famine, and disease. I ask a woman in Poli whether this year's harvest is exceptional. She says, "We are celebrating for two reasons: for the good harvest and for our children reaching adulthood."

I walk away with a renewed grasp of the essence of life.

Cuba:

In Cuba, a lot of things don't work as well as they should. A six-lane superhighway ends abruptly amid cane fields. Early-fifties Cadillacs, Chevies, Fords, DeSotos, Studebakers, and countless Ladas belch black smoke as they continue to transport Cubans. Overproduction of sugar cane depleted the country's fertile soil, and now Cuba must spend scarce hard currency to import food.

However, some things work quite well. Cuba has:

- the longest life expectancy of any country in Latin America,
- the best free medical care of any country in the Western hemisphere,
- a lower infant mortality rate than the United States,
- the most comprehensive free educational system in Latin America,
- almost 100 percent literacy,
- and nearly 100 percent electrification.

These are achievements of the 1959 Revolution. They help account for the massive public support for the Revolutionary government despite its mistakes, occasional corruption, and political heavy-handedness. But there is another seldom-examined achievement directly attributable to Cuban Socialism and the Revolution. Cuba has the most original, diverse, and thriving visual and performing arts of any country its size in the world.

It is this phenomenon that we, twelve American travelers, visit the island to observe in 2013. Barbara and I are last-minute additions, having been in Cameroon when the trip was first scheduled. Then Hurricane Sandy ravaged Cuba, and the trip was postponed, making it possible for us to sign up.

We embark on an Art and Architecture Tour, which qualifies as part of the "people-to-people" exception to the travel embargo. The tour is led by Sandra Levinson, Executive Director of the Center for Cuban Studies in New York. Sandy has made many trips to the island, speaks fluent Spanish, and has been a long-time supporter of Cuban artists. Her numerous contacts give us an inside track on Cuban art and politics. During the tour, we learn about not only Cuba's leading artists but also the art of leading Cuba.

Our group consists of twelve old and new friends. Four of us had been law partners and the others have a personal tie with one or another of us. We all share progressive political values.

Coming from as far away as New York, Michigan, and Hawaii, the group assembles in Miami on March 14, the day before our flight to Havana. We get up early the next day, anticipating a long line at the security check prior to boarding our two thirty p.m. flight. The wait is for our protection. I try not to think of Cubana Airlines Flight 455, blown up in 1976 by right-wing Cuban exiles.

The flight is uneventful. Everyone cheers as we touch down safely in Havana. A man sitting in front of Barbara weeps; he is visiting his family in Cuba for the first time in sixteen years.

Meeting us at the terminal is our in-country guide, Jesus Noguera, a cheerful, fit young man in his forties who speaks excellent English. We board a small tour bus and are driven along the Malecón, Havana's seaside jetty. It is lined with what appear to be deserted luxury apartments and mansions. A closer examination, however, reveals empty window frames draped with the clothes lines of squatters, less glamorous than the brocaded drapes of the buildings' prior, affluent residents. We pass the Nacional, one of a handful of old, classy hotels the government has allowed foreign investors to refurbish and manage. According to Jesus, Fidel welcomed tourists but eschewed heavy investment in tourism, regarding it as demeaning and a source of corruption, prostitution, and narcotics trafficking. Today, Raúl Castro sees it otherwise and is taking steps to upgrade tourist facilities and capture sorely needed hard currency. The Nacional itself was formerly part of the archipelago of hotels, showbars, casinos, and brothels controlled by Santos Trafficante Jr., Meyer Lansky, and others until 1959. These gangsters have long since been arrested and expelled from Cuba, and their property confiscated. The Nacional is still open, sans casino, but with Desi Arnaz–style floor shows called *tropicanas* for the tourists. We finally reach our accommodation, Hotel Saratoga, another elegant, old institution run by foreign investors.

On first impression, Havana seems to be a curious mix of the preserved and the neglected, the occupied and the abandoned. Almost all of the facades are painted in pastel colors—blue, green, yellow, orange, and pink—which glow in the afternoon sun. There are graceful neighborhoods with boulevards, lovely colonial homes, and well-tended parks. Havana has a funky Centro comprised of half-deserted Spanish-era public buildings (including the Capitol), some fortifications, and a few pedestrian streets with shops and bars. Some of the bars have signs claiming they were Hemingway hangouts. We soon learn that many of the "deserted" buildings in the Centro contain bustling studios, galleries, restaurants, night clubs, and bookstores.

Art is everywhere. It is in the day-glo colors of the lovingly maintained ancient cars on the roads. It is in parks, which are dotted with sculpture. It is found in formal venues like galleries and museums, or on signs and billboards. It is in the political graffiti on walls and music and dance in the streets. Here, art is an organic part of life. It is humorous as well—for instance, every morning, a man our age approaches a sculpture of John Lennon sitting on a park bench and puts a pair of round-framed glasses on Lennon's nose. He returns in the evening to remove them.

In our exploration of Cuban art, we notice that the shape of the island is a common motif. Other symbols or icons include the pattern and colors of the Cuban flag; the unmistakable likeness of the national hero, José Martí, with his waxed mustache; portraits of the revolutionary leaders Fidel, Raúl, and Che; Catholic and Santerian images; and themes of sexuality and gender.

Concentrating on Havana, Santiago, and surrounding areas, we visit the studios of a wide variety of artists. A one-hour bus ride from Havana brings us to the community of Las Terrazos, where farmers once sowed their crops on terraces in the hilly terrain. This idyllic, forested setting on a river in the San Rosario Hills is designated as an environmentally protected "biosphere" where only original residents and artists can live. Other Cubans may visit and picnic. It is no surprise that the artists in this community concentrate on pastoral settings and depictions of the flora and fauna around them. Lester Campa, a painter and printmaker, works with bark and driftwood. Jorge Duporte, a self-taught artist, specializes in precise Audubon-like paintings and drawings of plants and birds. Many of his botanicals relate to the novels of one of Cuba's most distinguished authors, Alejo Carpentier.

We visit Roberto Salas, whose father, Osvaldo, is renowned for his photographs of the Cuban Revolution. Osvaldo had daily access to Fidel, Che, Raúl, and other leaders both during and after the armed struggle and became known as the Revolution's unofficial photographer. Roberto followed in his father's footsteps and has published many photos in *Life* and other magazines. He shows us his remarkable black-and-white photographs—most of them portraits—and Barbara is ready to throw away her camera.

The home and studio of Alicia Leal and Juan Moreira is located on a tree-shaded street in Havana's Vedado district. Their art is highly symbolic, influenced by Hispanic and African cultures and incorporating Catholic, Santerian, and secular Cuban iconography. Leal's paintings, with their aura of mysticism, are often brightly colored images of women as well as explorations of sexuality. Moreira's work combines human figures with totems and idols.

In her small apartment, twenty-six-year-old avant-garde artist Mabel Poblet works on a large scale. She constructs self-portraits from tiny photos that, when arranged on a board the size of a ping-pong table, form the likeness of her face, with full red lips and long, black eyelashes. The effect is somewhat like a mosaic, but with the photos painstakingly raised on pins to create an illusion of depth. Her work is, implicitly, very sexy.

Some of the other pieces we saw were overtly sexual. On one occasion, I sat down on a chair to rest in the last gallery we visited at the end of a long day and smiled at Barbara as she snapped my picture. It was not until we looked at the photo a few hours later that we realized I was sitting in front of a large painting of female genitalia, with a big grin on my face.

Another significant feature we observed is how involved the artists are in their community and how much the community respects the value of art. Even artists with international reputations maintain ties to their neighborhood and provide support in the form of education, employment, or resources.

We find Sandra Dooley, who is Cuban of part-Scottish ancestry, in a sunlit seaside studio and home where she creates paintings and ceramics that are impressionistic and representational, many depicting Cuban folk tales and myths. Dooley hires local residents as assistants, encouraging the development of their artistic skills and displaying their artwork.

The hyperactive ceramicist José Rodriguez Fuster lives and works in the Jaimanitas district. In addition to a multitude of other civic projects, Fuster has adorned entire blocks of his neighborhood with tiles and mosaics, transforming it into an enchanted kingdom. He has created Gaudi-like towers, murals, giant chess sets, and waves of color on every surface of his garden walls, garage doors, gates, balconies, and roofs, as well as of those of his neighbors. The government turned him loose in Havana's Centro to perform his magic on various defunct buildings, and his murals enliven the walls of a local Vedado athletic complex.

We squeeze in a side trip to the barbershop and salon of Havana's premier hair stylist. Gilberto "Papito" Valladares is an artist of another sort, but no less an artist. His shop, on the third floor of a centuries-old building near the Malecón, is a dreamlike warren of rooms with eighteen-foot ceilings, walls covered with mirrors and paintings, and elaborate chandeliers. He shares his good fortune by teaching neighborhood residents hair-cutting and styling techniques—all for free. Papito also funds the art project Arte Corte for the benefit of the community. Outside his shop, a lively children's street theater supported by the project performs slapstick routines to the delight of dozens of youngsters.

Manuel Mendive, perhaps Cuba's best-known post-Revolution visual artist, makes a contribution to his community on several levels. He lives "in the country," a two-hour drive from Havana. When we arrive, we feel like we have been deposited in an artistic Shangri-La. His house is in a sprawling, thickly wooded compound with a view down a forested valley to the sea. Artwork fills two studios and decorates the grounds.

Manuel Mendive

Born in Cuba in 1944 to Afro-Cuban parents, Mendive received formal training at the Academy of San Alejandro in Havana. He departed from formalism to pursue themes and visions from African Yoruba culture and the Santeria religion. As a professional artist, he received a salary and free materials and supplies from a government arts agency. In turn, he gave some of the proceeds from the sale of his works to the agency. Now, his large-scale paintings and sculptures regularly bring in five-figure prices in US dollars. He employs many local residents as assistants and pays taxes.

Though Mendive could live anywhere in the world, he is committed to Cuba. A work of art himself, he is of imposing size, with a dramatic ebony face, silver-gray beard, and dreadlocks. He wears a white muslin dashiki. Hollywood could cast him as a black Moses were it not for his cheerful good humor and ever-present smile.

All this art did not appear spontaneously. Cuba has devoted considerable resources to formal art education. The Instituto Superior de Arte (ISA) in Havana is the premier college for five career paths: Music, Visual Arts, Theatre Arts, Dance Arts, and Arts and Audiovisual Communication Media. Award-winning buildings on the main campus in Havana are round-domed, breast-like units, connected by loggia and interspersed with pools and sculpture in shapes suggestive of the female body. Tuition is free, and admission is highly competitive. The campus sits on the former golf course that belonged to a racially segregated pre-Revolution country club, which even dictator Fulgencio Batista could not join because his skin was a couple of shades too dark. The present student body is a healthy mix of gender and skin color, from café au lait to espresso.

In Santiago, students from the Casa José María Heredia School for the Arts—an elementary and high school devoted to music and the performing arts—perform for us for two hours. We are treated to a Handel saxophone solo, a Brahms piano solo, and a quartet of ten-year-olds singing, of all things, "Give Me That Old Time Religion." Traditional Cuban and jazz dances are also performed. At the end, the students drag us onto the floor to dance and make fools of ourselves. They take many pictures of our awkward display with their phones. What particularly struck us was not only the energy and high spirits of the students but also the camaraderie and mutual support between the faculty and their pupils.

Instituto Superior de Arte, Havana

Ballet students, Casa José María Heredia School for the Arts, Santiago

Folk dancers, Casa José María Heredia School for the Arts, Santiago

However, because of the blockade and embargo, musical instruments and accessories in Cuba are scarce. Students who play wind instruments have to share one reed among the whole class. Dance students have to make do with broken-in or worn-out shoes—or none at all.

One of our most remarkable encounters was with a collective of artists who reject formal art education. These naive or self-taught painters live in the sugar mill town of Mella, near Santiago. The collective, Grupo Bayate, was founded in the 1990s by Luis Rodriguez Arias, also known as *El Maestro*. His son, Luis Rodriguez Ricardo, who calls himself *El Estudiante,* now leads the collective. It consists of eight or nine artists who dispense with techniques such as perspective and instead concentrate on depictions of their lives, culture, work, recreation, and surroundings. Their paintings emphasize the blazing colors of the fields, hills, and rivers, with special attention to the thousands of shades of green of the forest. Some works strongly resemble the jungle paintings of the French Impressionist Henri Rousseau, who was also referred to as a "primitive" or "naive" artist.

The members of the group have varied backgrounds. El Maestro was a baker. El Estudiante earned a degree in highway construction. Others in the collective worked in the sugar mill or as policemen, lawyers, or doctors. Most continue in their regular jobs. Rousseau also had a day job. He was a customs officer.

Santiago is a beautiful Spanish colonial city on the eastern end of the island. Because of its history as a crossroads port, the architecture in Santiago is a varied combination of Spanish Colonial, Moorish, French, Italian, and Chinese elements.

On October 12, 2012, Hurricane Sandy passed directly over the city, causing nine deaths, destroying fifteen thousand homes, and tearing apart countless roofs and trees. Sandy was the worst hurricane to hit Santiago in one hundred years. Cubans were upset by the loss of life, which was unusually high. Santiago's recovery, however, far outpaced that of New York City after Sandy.

As of our visit in March 2013, power has been restored, businesses have reopened, and repairs are well under way. However, only

Street musicians, Santiago

stumps remain where most trees stood. The city looks as if it has just gotten a meteorological buzz cut.

Santiago is also known for its significant revolutionary history. It is the location of the tomb of José Martí, the Moncado Barracks where the first shots of the Revolution were fired in 1953, and the City Hall balcony where Fidel announced the triumph of the Revolution in 1959.

Politics is as omnipresent as art. The two are interrelated, not only in the work of individual artists, but also in the public space. The roads we travel are devoid of commercial billboards. Instead, colorful and eye-catching political messages urge Cubans to support the Revolution, build socialism, fight corruption, increase production, mourn Chávez, and demand the release and return of the "Cuban Five" political prisoners then held in Florida.

Though virtually unknown in the US, the "Cuban Five" are considered heroes in Cuba. In 1976, Cubana Airlines Flight 455 was bombed, killing all seventy-three people on board. Authorities in the

Castro government had reason to believe that organizations of right-wing Cubans living in Miami had planned and carried out the attack. Cuba made a formal request to the FBI to investigate, but the request was ignored. Five Cuban intelligence officers infiltrated the suspect organizations and obtained evidence that implicated Luis Posada, a Cuban exile and former CIA operative. When the Cuban Five presented a dossier of their findings to the Justice Department, the FBI arrested them on charges of Conspiracy to Engage in Espionage. They were convicted in 2001 in the extremely hostile venue of south Florida and sentenced to imprisonment of forty years to life. Luis Posada was never arrested or indicted.

· We have several frank political exchanges with Cubans, but one that stands out takes place in the living room of José "Pepe" Raúl Viera Linares, the first Deputy Minister of Foreign Affairs from 1981 to 1990.

Pepe invites the thirteen of us into his modest home in Havana, where we discuss Cuban and US politics and economics. His wife, Maria Cecilia Bermudez, serves coffee and cookies and joins the group. Pepe worked for the Revolution in many leadership capacities, including serving as legal counsel to the Cuban Mission to the United Nations.

During our conversation, he frequently refers to the "Economic and Social Policy Guidelines for the Party and the Revolution," a nineteen-page, single-spaced document finalized in 2011 after two years of debate. Pepe explains that the Guidelines outline how Cuba should cautiously begin a transition to a mixed economy with a greater role for private enterprise, while the government retains control of the major means of production, financial institutions, and overall socialist planning.

When members of our group raise questions about one-party rule and censorship, Pepe responds, "These measures were justified for a long time because of the imminent threat of forcible intervention by the United States. That danger is now greatly diminished."

"What next?" I ask. "Where does Cuba go?" "The role of government is to provide an economic system that is attractive to the people," he replies. "In April, 1961, Cuba chose socialism. Now they want a mixed economy, and the Party is reluctant to move."

Pepe is concerned that the Guidelines are just that—guidelines, not laws. The mixed economy envisioned in the document will require laws governing labor relations, property transfer, and bankruptcy. He has confidence in Raúl Castro's abilities, but there will be tough times ahead as the Government sheds as many as 250,000 jobs. Pepe looks tired and sad. He has spent his life struggling to attain a humane, socialist Cuba. I imagine that he is afraid that his dream may be replaced by a society of consumerism, inequality, and exploitation. And there is nothing he can do about it.

Cutbacks may affect funding for the arts as well. I only hope that this will not result in fewer ISA's and Casa José María Heredia schools and more tropicana floor shows.

In Santiago, we also meet with members of a Committee for the Defense of the Revolution (CDR) in a neighborhood close to our hotel. The entire community—about one hundred adults and children—show up to welcome us. The gathering is held under a streetlight where they hold CDR meetings every other month. There is music, dancing, and food. Children recite poems and sing songs about José Martí.

We are free to talk to anyone we want about any topic, and so our conversations center around the "Cuban Five," the post-Sandy cleanup, and the new Guidelines.

I find myself in a small group talking about the Guidelines. I ask whether they had a chance to consider a draft of the document before it was adopted and if they were opposed to its provisions. The locals reply that they reviewed it thoroughly and authorized their City Council representative to convey their approval. They did so even though they were aware that its implementation would result in job losses, perhaps including their own or their neighbors'. A woman says in English, "It has to be done. The country cannot go on as it is. We will survive it."

"How was your representative chosen?" I ask. She replies, "Candidates posted one-page résumés on a fence, and the CDR voted at the next meeting." Membership in the Cuban Communist Party is not a requirement.

We're impressed by the solidarity of the community and their support for one another and their country.

What we saw and heard in Cuba was a sampling of the explosion of Cuban art and culture since 1959. This development is all the more remarkable in an economy of scarcity. It is the result of the decision by the revolutionary government to prioritize artistic expression.

Cuban Socialism is designed with the understanding that meeting basic human physical needs and providing an equitable system of wealth distribution is necessary, though not sufficient, for most people—at least, not indefinitely. The goal is the creation of optimum conditions for individual and collective human development and expression. Cuba has come a long way toward making life worth living through creative thought and activity, both for the artist and society.

In the last fifty years, the Cuban people have made great strides in the critical areas of health, medical services, education, literacy, the arts, and other basic human needs. For example, there is CENESEX, a robust organization that advocates for gay rights in the machismo culture of Latin America. Founded shortly after the Revolution by The Federation of Cuban Women, it promotes sex education through dissemination of information, training of medical professionals, and social activism. Sex education is a matter of state policy, and the focus is on safe sex rather than abstinence. CENESEX also deals with the issues of access to abortion (which is legal within the first ten weeks of pregnancy), homophobia, HIV treatment, and LGBT rights.

Cubans have successfully resisted the overt and covert attempts by the United States to effect "regime change." They defend their island and their social achievements. They have already survived the ill-fated, US-sponsored Bay of Pigs invasion and the years of shortages and hardship caused by the breakup of the Soviet Union.

Now, having made these sacrifices, Cubans want more of the consumer goods and services that we in America take for granted—the kind that small neighborhood enterprises best provide, such as groceries, shoe repair, auto repair, plumbing, carpentry, art supplies, school supplies, and dry cleaning. They want more and better food. Many are already ahead of the government, offering products and services without the sanction of the state, creating an underground economy. Per the Guidelines, the government is moving to stimulate and encourage small businesses and private or cooperative agriculture. But this takes time. Which leads them to the more immediate payoff of tourism.

In 2012, largely because of educational people-to-people exchanges and the relaxation of travel restrictions for Cuban families, more than ninety-eight thousand US citizens visited Cuba according to Reuters, spending hard currency. If all restrictions are lifted, many more Americans could be expected to visit, providing Cuba with the capital needed to hold civil society together while transitioning to a mixed economy—but at a price.

On our last night, we attend a farewell dinner at Parador La Guardia, a restaurant catering to tourists. We think about the ordinary Cubans who work there but can't afford to eat there.

During the long, dark walk back to the hotel through foggy, dimly lit streets, we see open transactions of prostitution and drug sales in cars and on foot. I wonder if the sellers would be there at all if not for the proximity of tourists with hard currency. Certainly, if we know what is happening, the police must, too. However, there is no police presence.

We recall Fidel's warning about tourism.

Epilogue

On July 20, 2015, fifty-four years after diplomatic ties were suspended, Cuba and the United States resumed diplomatic relations and have since reopened their respective embassies in Havana and Washington, DC. The United States has not lifted the trade embargo or relinquished control of Guantanamo Bay.

Since we left Cuba, all of the "Cuban Five" have returned to the island. The final three were released in a prisoner exchange in 2014.

Politically and economically, Cuba is at a critical juncture in its struggle to maintain a humane socialist economy and civil society—and we're convinced the Cuban people will work it out.

Sing-sing in Palombei, Sepik River, Papua New Guinea

Sing-sing in Angorogho, Tufi, Papua New Guinea

Facial tattoos, Tufi, Papua New Guinea

City view of Algiers, Algeria

Lone Tuareg, Algeria

Assekrem, Algeria

Ghardia, M'zab, Algeria

Kathmandu, Nepal

Buddhist shrine on trail to Laurebina Yak, Nepal

Chitwan, Nepal

Baka hunter, Cameroon

Bamileke king and his third wife, Cameroon

M'bororo woman, Cameroon

Proud Baka father and son, Cameroon

Street scene in Havana, Cuba

Mabel Poblet in her studio, Havana, Cuba

Home studio of Alicia Leal and Juan Moreira, Havana, Cuba

Dogon masked dance ceremony, Tireli, Mali

Mosque and market, Djenné, Mali

Leopard slayer, Mali

Persepolis, Iran

Khaju Bridge, Isfahan, Iran

Imam Square, Sheikh Lotfollah Mosque, Isfahan, Iran

Dusk on the Orinoco River, Venezuela

Young Yanomami chief, the Orinoco River, Venezuela

Yanomami family, the Orinoco River, Venezuela

American International School, Gaza Strip, State of Palestine

Children of Johr al-Deek, Gaza Strip, State of Palestine

Woman with tattoos, Ethiopia

Surmi woman and child, Omo Valley, Ethiopia

The bull jump, Hamer Village, Ethiopia

Mali:

Disregarding the State Department's Travel Advisory List (i.e., "don't go there"), we travel to Mali, in West Africa, in February, 2012. There is some skirmishing in the north between nomadic Tuareg separatists (MNLA) seeking their own nation and the Malian army. A few foreign tourists have been taken hostage. Certain towns, including Timbuktu, are, for practical purposes, inaccessible. We did not plan to visit Timbuktu, so this is not a deterrent. Its historic cachet notwithstanding, Timbuktu is half covered with sand from the encroaching Sahara. Nor are we planning to visit the Tuareg settlements in the north, since we had already spent time with the Tuareg in southern Algeria in October, 2011.

Instead, we focus on Central Mali, the most fertile section of the country, watered by the Niger and its tributaries. Along these rivers are the port cities of Ségou, Mopti, Djenné, and Bamako, each with a centuries-old culture. Our plan is to trek through the villages of the Dogon people who live, as they have for a thousand years, in the Bandiagara Escarpment, the nearly inaccessible cliffs that drop sharply to form the edge of the Dogon plateau. Also on our itinerary is Le Festival sur le Niger, an annual world music festival in Ségou, featuring musicians from all over Africa.

Mali is one of the poorest countries in the world. In contrast to its neighbor, Algeria, which has an abundance of oil and natural gas, Mali has an abundance of onions and mangoes. Its officialdom is as corrupt as any on the planet. Millions of dollars in UN and NGO civil and military aid has been diverted to the coffers of ranking civilian and military leaders.

A preview of Mali's penurious state is its Permanent Mission to the United Nations in New York City, where we must go to obtain a tourist visa. The Mission is a tiny two-room walk-down in a fashionable district in Manhattan. A waiting area with folding chairs is separated by a glass shield from the working space of the Mission's single employee, Madame X, a robust, friendly woman and Jacqueline of all trades. There is no security guard. Jacqueline extracts the visa fee from each of us, has us fill out a short form, receives our inoculation records, and advises us that the visas will issue in one week (they do)—all within fifteen minutes. Two other applicants await her services, amiable and scruffy young American men looking forward to total immersion in the Festival on the Niger. They are also processed with dispatch. The modest facade of Mali's Mission belies its professional and efficient operation.

Bamako

Arriving in Bamako late at night, we deplane onto the still-warm tarmac and lug our carry-on backpacks into a crowded, stifling terminal. Waving a sign with our names is Adama, our guide. Most Malians speak French, but Adama also speaks excellent English, as well as Bambara (the most prevalent non-European language in Mali), Dogon, and others. He is a garrulous, athletic young man in his late twenties who seems to know everyone in Bamako. He is Dogon, his kin residing in various parts of the Escarpment.

The hotel is modern, with functioning air conditioning and a pool suitable for lap swimming—factors that take on importance in the sub-Saharan heat.

Our pre-breakfast walk takes us along the Avenue of Ministries, a boulevard constructed by the French during colonial times. We dodge motorbikes and broken sidewalk tiles. Many uniformed personnel, most without weapons, stand around, chatting. The various Ministries of the Malian government along the Avenue are in states of neglect and disrepair.

After breakfast, Adama drives us to a viewpoint where we can see most of Bamako. The dusty dun-colored city of one million people sprawls over the flood plain of the Niger. Colorful relief is provided by vegetable and flower gardens and mango groves in strips of green along the riverbanks. There are few buildings over three stories tall. Our viewing site, according to Adama, is the Malian Army Commando Training Center, with climbing structures and an obstacle course made of used tires and railroad ties. It looks like an elementary school playground. The Center is vacant. The treeless slopes of the hill are littered with trash. Shredded pieces of black plastic shopping bags cling to fences and low-lying bushes, like flocks of emaciated crows.

Next, we drive to the Bamako Recycling Market, a remarkable place. Acres of sheds made of corrugated steel roof held up by old pipes and crooked sticks shelter men who are cutting and welding auto and machine parts. Disabled vehicles do not litter the landscape in Mali. They are brought here, chopped into parts, and sold. Whatever cannot be restored to its original function is worked into some handy implement—a bucket, wheelbarrow, rake, machete, scythe, scoop, or piece of furniture. Nothing is wasted. It is the ultimate recycling center.

The sheds are hot under the metal roofs, and the men's work is hard and dangerous. Barefoot, wearing nothing but shorts, and without goggles or masks, the men wield cutting and welding torches hooked up to battered tanks of fuel. Radios blare popular music, and laughter is heard all around.

The finished parts and implements are stacked in a neat array for inspection and sale on the street that traverses the market. On

115

this same street is the principal fresh food market for Bamako. It is as devoid of men as the welding sheds are of women—Malian women are in charge here.

The women in Mali are tall, with erect postures from a lifetime of balancing impossible loads on their heads while a baby is slung on their backs. Many wear traditional dresses called *boubous* with matching turbans in bold patterns and bright harmonious colors, vivid against their dark skin. The women we meet are assertive but good-humored, liking nothing better than a ribald story or raucous joke. Their domestic chores are endless and tiresome but are done communally amid much gossip and teasing.

Our lunch at a Senegalese restaurant consists of a fish stew made with the ubiquitous river fish, *capitaine*, which is served a dozen different ways during our trip. I never tire of it.

We visit the National Museum and Park, a green, verdant oasis in the dry urban expanse of Bamako. The museum is empty, perhaps because there is an admission fee. Exquisite icons, masks, and statues from all over Mali are beautifully displayed, with explanations in both French and English. Outside the museum, a small World Music concert led by local musicians attracts a crowd. Malians of all ages get up and dance.

The Grand Marche (big market) is bustling in the late afternoon. Everything is for sale, including traditional remedies for physical, mental, and spiritual maladies. Ingredients include monkey and fox skulls, skins and furs, and roots and mushrooms.

At night, we stroll the crowded streets of Bamako without incident or fear. The next day, Barbara gets lost during an early morning walk but finds the hotel after a lot of signing and pointing by friendly locals.

Ségou

One hour after we begin the six-hour drive to Ségou, we have to stop. There is a problem with the Land Cruiser's brakes. We wait in the sun for a replacement auto; no point in complaining. At last, a car arrives, and we continue to Ségou. It is Mali's second city, with a more laid-back atmosphere than Bamako, which is already pretty relaxed. We stay in a modest two-story establishment with a pleasant courtyard dining area and café serving beer, pizza, and capitaine to Malians, ex-pats, and a few tourists.

Ségou is the site of the annual World Music Festival on the Niger, for which we have VIP passes. It is held in an open-air arena on the waterfront, with an enormous stage, screen, and sound system, as well as ground level seating of about an acre and a grandstand at the back.

By nightfall, the dusty street next to the hotel is packed with Malians, other West Africans, young Europeans, and a few Americans. We bring up the average age on the street by several years. Adama guides us through the throngs and into the roped-off VIP grandstand. Even these VIP seats are far from the stage, but the screen provides close-ups of the performers. The arena is filled to capacity, and people are listening in the streets and in boats on the river.

The music has already started. It can probably be heard in neighboring Burkina Faso. There is no music program, and Adama, who has ducked out to take care of other business, is not around to translate the band announcements made in French and Bambara. The music is great, mostly a mix of West African traditional percussion and song, with occasional elements of blues, house, hip-hop, folk, and rock.

An assortment of suits and embroidered boubous sit in the grandstand, chatting with one another while the bands, the soloists, and the audience go wild. We stay, enjoying the music and spectacle for about two hours, and then, still jet-lagged, retire for the day. The beats and rhythms continue to throb into the small hours of the morning.

The performers are all Malian on our second night. Some of the lyrics are in English and overtly political. Rokia Traore sings "Africa United" like an anthem, its background rhythms bringing the young fans to their feet.

The Bandiagara Escarpment: Home of the Dogon

The Bandiagara Escarpment is a seven-hour drive north of Ségou. On the way, we stop at a Bou village to view their millet storage silos and cylindrical huts with pointed thatched roofs that are clustered together like a mute, miniature town. We pass calabash farms, where Fulani women carry loads of mangoes on their heads. The driver takes the Land Cruiser off road for many miles, arriving at last at a small Dogon village set in a crevice of a hill on the Dogon Plateau. It is the village of Adama's grandfather, now deceased. One of Adama's uncles still lives there.

As we approach the village, walking beside onion and millet fields, Adama and the people we encounter exchange greetings in the Dogon manner. This is a ritual that takes place between all Dogon at every meeting, even between people who have seen one another earlier that same day. Adama observes this ritual scrupulously. The oldest begins the exchange with "*Aga po seo?*" (Hello, how are you?). Next comes "*Oumana seo?*" (How is the family?), "*Ounou seo?*" (How are the children?), and "*Yahana go seo?*" (How is the spouse?). The reply to each question is *seo*, meaning *okay*. The exchange is then reversed, and the younger greeter makes the inquiries as the older replies, "*Seo.*" The recitation is done almost simultaneously and usually takes less than a minute, but it requires the speakers to stop and acknowledge one another's presence and worth as an individual and member of the Dogon community. The back-and-forth nature of these greetings reminds us of the call and response of African-American gospel music.

A climb up the rocks, through narrow passageways and up ladders made of logs notched with foot holds, leads us to a tiny courtyard where Adama's uncle and his family reside. There are very few people in the village. Most are in the fields on the Plateau, in school, or sleeping in the cool darkness of the windowless rooms carved out of the rock and lined with hardened mud. Adama's uncle invites us into his rooms. On display are copies of Dogon totems and icons as well as contemporary animal and human figures, carved for sale to tourists in the cities. Upon inquiry he brings out some original, antique figures, which have apparently been in the community for years. We select and bargain for two, a two-foot-high bearded and seated elderly male and a small female figure. While we are aware that we have been guided to the uncle's home in the hope of a sale, we don't mind contributing to the community.

Most of the structures in Dogon villages are rectangular in shape. There is a building for meetings of the elders and a town square for community meetings. An open pavilion covered by a low thatched roof is used as a venue for adversaries to present their arguments and resolve disputes in a court of elders. The low roof requires everyone involved to sit or squat, emphasizing their equality before the tribunal.

It is the weekly market day in Niangono, and, as usual, the women are in charge. Amid the press of the crowded lanes between vendors, I make the mistake of stepping over a cookpot tended by a market matron who immediately scolds me in a loud voice about my

Street in Dogon village

Meeting house, Dourou

breach of etiquette. My embarrassment entertains the surrounding sales force. I apologize profusely, to no avail.

We spend the night in the city of Bandiagara near the edge of the Escarpment. The only other dinner guests in the café are a German couple who are here to help build a school in the city.

Near the edge of the Dogon Plateau, we begin a four-kilometer trek down a fault in the Escarpment to the Dogon village of Nambori. The trail traverses the broken head and face of the cliff, follows dry streambeds, and descends into steep claustrophobic gorges, some only one-meter wide. After two hours, we emerge from the shadow of a gorge onto the Gondo Plain at the base of the cliff.

Stretching to the southeast, the plain is classic African savannah, covered with dry, dusty grass. Baobab trees are silhouetted against serrated clouds above a distant mountain ridge, like birds on a wire. Facing the cliff, well-tended fields of rice, sorghum, millet, and onion are enclosed by bamboo poles entwined with branches of thorn trees. Rising from the plain about one quarter of the way up a five-hundred-meter

120

cliff is Nambori. Square-peaked silos mix with adobe houses that are the same ochre shade as the cliffs, a monochrome Cubist assemblage.

Above the Dogon buildings are abandoned dwellings dug into the cliff face, as well as square and round towers with windows, doorways, ladders, and roofs. These were the homes of the Tellem, a people who preceded the Dogon as occupants of the Escarpment seven or eight hundred years ago. Under pressure from the more numerous farming Dogon, these hunter-gatherers moved over the Escarpment onto the Plateau, where they still live in small communities. The Dogon use the former Tellem dwellings for burial sites and storage of secret society artifacts. Above the Tellem towers, about three-quarters of the way up the cliff face, is a line of tiny caves—holes in the soft rock. These caves were occupied and then abandoned by a Pygmy people who arrived before the Tellem and who long ago migrated to the forests of central Africa. We like to think that the Baka we visited in Cameroon are their descendants.

Remains of Tellem and Pygmy villages, Escarpment

The Tellem and Pygmy sites appear at regular intervals along the entire two-hundred-kilometer length of the Escarpment. It is like the Mesa Verde ruins in Colorado, just twenty times as long.

We move slowly, taking in the haunting beauty of this primeval scene. The spell is broken as we approach the cultivated fields and come across two young women working the soil. Adama hails them and the *seo* greetings ensue. He teases and flirts for a while, making them laugh, before introducing us. He then leads us on the long climb through twisting lanes and stairways to the top tier of the Nambori village, where we are to stay the night. A meal of chicken and vegetables in onion sauce is waiting for us.

Adama informs us that some young people of the village would like to perform a wedding dance for us, but the standard fee is equivalent to seventy-five dollars and there are no other tourists to split the costs. However, we have come all this way to see artistic and cultural expressions unique to Mali, in particular those of the Dogon, so we agree to the proposal.

An hour after nightfall, we are led to a small square lined with benches in a corner of the village. A crowd of about seventy villagers assembles, most in their twenties and thirties, some forming a circle. Many of the women wear traditional indigo boubous. A percussion ensemble of five or six older men begins to warm up. The rhythms are hypnotic, seemingly repetitive but with small episodic changes that gradually alter the whole rhythmic pattern.

A young man in slacks and a white shirt and a young woman in a boubou walk into the center of the space as the rhythms slow down. Barefoot, side-by-side, they shuffle slowly on the hard-packed earth, moving forward with small, hesitation steps. Suddenly, the drummers accelerate the pace and increase the volume. The dancers drop into a semicrouch, knees bent, head up, arms straight out in front, feet pounding the earth in double time—an explosion of energy for twenty seconds until the drums relent and the dancers resume the slow shuffle for several minutes. This sequence repeats four or five times until the dance is over. It is a traditional dance performed by young people who have decided to wed—their public performance together an announcement to the village of their engagement status.

Everyone, many long married with children, takes their turn on the floor, showing that they can still perform this demanding percussive dance. Adama, a real athlete, does back flips in his rendition. Finally, they drag us onto the floor where we perform a feeble version of the dance, evoking applause and laughter.

Our sleeping quarters are on the roof of the chief's house. The roof is lightly covered with clean sand, a mosquito net is strung over some rope, and floor mats and pillows are provided.

Just before we fall asleep, a strong male voice resonates across the rooftops in the slow, distinctive tones of the Dogon language, speaking for several minutes. He is the village crier, announcing the death of an elderly man. "That is why the Chief was not at the dance," Adama explains to us. "He had to preside over preburial rituals."

The call of several roosters wakes us at four a.m. We walk downhill through Nambori, greet some residents working in the fields, and continue our trek along the base of the Escarpment to Tireli, a sizeable village in the shadow of the cliffs. We have come to see a performance of the Sigi ritual.

The Sigi fits into Dogon mythology as a rite of atonement and initiation for male youths. The Dogon have a complicated creation myth in which young men engaged in some mischief, disrupting the creation of the earth. The disruption was overcome by the deities, but gods don't forget, so every sixty years, men wearing masks representing animals, humans, and spirits perform a dance of expiation. The sixty years coincides with the orbital cycle of Sirius, the Dog Star, the Dogon's most revered celestial object. We will be watching an authentic presentation, but not the real event.

On one side of a dusty ten-meter square, five men wielding small hammers beat out a rhythm on the stretched skin of log drums. Coming down a narrow lane is a contingent of masked and costumed figures, some with animal faces, some with tall headdresses rising straight up from their masks, some on stilts, and some wearing double-crossed white wooden slats on their heads. Groups of three or four wearing the same costume enter the square in single file, using little hopping steps. Each group in turn dances in unison. Those with towering headpieces whip their necks back and forth and in circles, their headgear skimming the sandy floor, raising dust clouds around their legs. The figures on stilts lurch from side to side. Some impersonate women involved in the myth, wearing coconut shell bras with sea shell–lined straps and straw skirts. Throughout, the drumming continues, seeming to echo the rhythm of my heart. I am overwhelmed by the drumbeat, the colors, the dance and the dust, and the simple fact of where I am. I don't want it to end.

Our trek through Dogon country takes four days and winds through several villages. Sometimes we have to cross courtyards, interrupting people working or relaxing together. Adama exchanges greetings with them in the *seo* manner, and they respond as a chorus. He tells them who we are and where we come from, and we pass out kola nuts as an apology for the intrusion. Kola nuts, when chewed, have a mild narcotic effect, and, to our lasting regret, we never tried them.

Later, we meet the district director of the local schools. The district has been hard hit by the drop-off in tourism caused by the skirmishing between the Tuareg and government troops in the north. The director explains that in Mali everything is privatized and expensive—higher education, medicine, health care, electricity. We feel helpless. All we can do is leave boxes of pencils for the students.

Farther along the Escarpment, the trail leads up the cliff to the remote village of Yougou Dougourou. This is where the real Sigi ceremony takes place, sans tourists. It is also where Dogon adolescent boys go into seclusion with village elder men, learn about Dogon myths and legends, and are circumcised, remaining in seclusion until they heal. The chief shows us the flat ledges on the cliffs where the boys are taught. Pictographs of animals, reptiles, humans, and imaginary creatures cover the walls of the ledges. The figures are stark red and black, outlined against a white background, extending thirty feet along the walls. Many have been restored, but the originals go back hundreds of years.

We continue our journey, scrambling up narrow gorges and log ladders to the top of the Escarpment. The summit is a moonscape of black rock, splintered and divided by sudden crevices. It affords a sweeping view of the Plain below. While we wander the strange surface, a dapper figure in a bright-blue jacket and yellow pants appears out of the gorge. The sudden and unexpected appearance of a brightly colored human presence in this monochromatic, desolate landscape is startling. He is a French engineer, donating his time and talent to repairing a dam for the village. He is all business and leaves after a few minutes, eager to get on with his work.

Entrance to the circumcision chamber, Yougou Dougourou, Cameroon

On the way down, we hear eerie, high-pitched sounds of distress. The cries get louder as we continue on the trail, and we come upon two large dogs, shaking and howling, trussed up in baskets guarded by two men. Adama hustles us past without greeting the men, which is unusual. He is appalled. "These dogs are to be sacrificed," he says, "but I know of no Dogon rite that calls for such slaughter." Stunned, we ask his advice as to what to do. Although distraught and angry, he murmurs, "Best not to interfere." We never learn the reason for this sacrifice. The sounds and images remain with us to this day.

After hiking out of the Escarpment, we spend the night in a hotel with a real bed, shower, and toilet for the first time in five days.

Mopti and Djenné

While we were in Ségou for the music festival, Adama had approached us with a serious expression. "We need to talk," he said. Karen, his boss at the travel agency, had called to tell him that the fighting in the north threatened to spread to areas near Mopti and Djenné, cities we planned to visit. She thought we should avoid that part of the country. Adama asked what we wanted to do. It didn't take us long to decide, perhaps naively, that we were willing to take the risk and continue the trip as planned. Even at our age, we think we are indestructible. And so, we travel on.

Mopti is a bustling harbor on a tributary of the Niger. The most common river craft is the pinnace, a wooden, shallow-draft boat ranging from ten to fifteen meters in length. It is powered by a small outboard motor with a long drive shaft extending from the stern to a tiny propeller. The pilot moves the drive shaft back and forth to steer, allowing the propeller to bounce over the many sandbars in the shallow river. Pilots sometimes put up sails made of stitched-together garbage bags.

In a boatyard on the riverbank, craftsmen in an enormous shed use hand tools to build the pinnaces. Again, nothing is wasted—scrap wood is carved into paddles, canes, toys, and ornaments. These graceful crafts can carry up to 150 metric tons. On the river, we see pinnaces overloaded with new bedroom sets, chairs, tables, and other furniture—to be delivered to weddings in Mopti so couples can immediately set up housekeeping.

A trip up the Bani in a pinnace brings us to a Fulani village. On the way, Adama points out a two-meter-long black snake swimming nearby. It's a cobra—a good swimmer. We take pictures but give it a wide berth.

The Fulani are principally herders and have close relations with the Dogon. Fulani women wear brightly patterned boubous with matching headscarves. They are friendly and have beautiful smiles, which are accentuated by black tattoos encircling their mouths. When we arrive, most of the women are washing clothes in the shallow water by the riverbank, gossiping and laughing together while their children splash and play happily among them.

The Fulani are known for their jolly courtship ritual in which young men, wearing conical hats and black makeup to emphasize their white teeth and eyes, do a shuffling, grinning, hand-clapping line dance, while young women stroll in front of the line and pick out the man they are interested in. In contrast to most Western dating

Fulani women, Mopti

rituals, there is no privacy here. The entire community has an interest in making sure matches are made as smoothly as possible.

Dinner is *poisson yassa*, a Senegalese dish, made with—what else—capitaine.

A short distance from Mopti is Djenné, the oldest urban site in West Africa. Ruins of a trading post just outside the city date back to 250 BC. An archeological dig sits at the original site. The dig ran out of money in the 1990s, and the only official evidence of its existence is a small sign. We wander unsupervised over two or three acres, picking up ancient pottery shards marked with crisscross designs. No one else is in sight. We replace the shards and drive off.

The Hotel Djenné Djenno is a small architectural marvel run by Sophie, a Swede married to a Malian. Separated from the teeming market city by a wide wadi or dry river, the hotel integrates the minimalist mud structure typical of Djenné into a spacious flower garden courtyard seamed with paths and shaded by palm trees.

At dusk, Sophie serves mimosas on the roof of the hotel. Merchants for Djenné's Monday market begin to arrive in donkey carts, horse drawn wagons, autos, and trucks, as well as on bicycles, horseback, and foot. They travel the road on the other side of the wadi as far as the eye can see. It is an otherworldly scene: a slow, silent procession silhouetted against the pastel-pink sunset.

We enjoy a Malian meal of stewed beef and beans, gazpacho, and ginger ice cream, while fourteen Latvians, fellow guests, hold raucous court amid the flower beds.

By dawn, hundreds of buyers and sellers fill the square in front of the Great Mosque in Djenné. The market is a crazy quilt of tents and shelters—a cacophony of haggling, a hustling and bustling hive of humanity. A political candidate holds a rally on a side street. Grizzled old hunters fire antique muskets into the dusty blue sky, and boys dance in unison to the beat of a single drum. Horses and donkeys are harnessed in a feedlot nearby. We weave in and out of the market's narrow lanes, importuned on all sides by vendors of everything from parrots to parsnips.

The Great Mosque looms over the market. It is a huge Afro-Gothic mud structure, the largest mud mosque in the world, its three towers rising eighteen meters above the square. Constructed in 1907, it looks like a cross between the Houses of Parliament and the Alamo. Non-Muslims have been barred from the interior ever since a French photographer used it as background for a fashion shoot.

As the day winds down, we return to the hotel for dinner and drinks, sitting again on the roof and watching the last of the merchants leave town, the procession a mirror image of the night before.

Bamako Redux

We return to Bamako after a seven-hour drive in stifling heat with no air conditioning. That evening, when our cab driver gets lost on our way to dinner, we approach several young men who have congregated near the unlit thoroughfares, talking and joking, seemingly at loose ends. They are friendly and helpful, but I wonder what they think of us, heirs to opportunities they can only imagine, yet asking them for help.

On our last day in Mali, we explore the hills outside Bamako, where there is a natural stone arch and cave important to Dogon mythology. Supposedly, an evil king was killed by a hero at the site of the arch, sometime before the Dogon moved off the plateau and onto the Escarpment. Sacrifices are still made in the cave to mollify the spirits.

On the way back to Bamako, we stop to see an old hunter who had killed a leopard that was a threat to the village's precious livestock. The villagers are proud of this feat, but he has to be coaxed out of his house to meet us. He wears his headdress adorned with the leopard's teeth and patiently poses for pictures. He shows us his weapon—a single-shot, hand-made rifle, which is notoriously inaccurate. He must have had to get very close in order to kill the big cat. I come away with admiration for the old man's courage, but also with sadness at the death of this magnificent creature, which was only trying to survive, just as were the villagers.

Before we leave the village, we hang out in the square, observing two women in boubous pound millet, driving thick mortar poles deep into a narrow pestle of wood, rhythmically alternating two-handed downstrokes. This is physically demanding work, requiring both strength and precise timing. The women, talking and laughing, one with a baby strapped to her back, keep at it for an hour, We're impressed by the apparent ease and good humor with which they perform this task. Any personal trainer in the US would be proud to have such clients. The millet pounders are still at it when we leave.

At seven p.m., we leave for the airport and the trip home.

"So," I ask Adama, "do you have another tour lined up?"

"No," he says. "There aren't any, because of the fighting in the north."

"What will you do?"

"I am qualified as a welder, but I need to raise eight hundred dollars for an electrical hookup to my shop."

"Can't your father help? You have a wife and family to support."

"No," Adama says, "My father has three wives and families to support. And I can't get a loan because I am not a government employee."

Eight hundred dollars seems far too much for a mere electrical hookup, even in Brooklyn. Is some of it needed for bribes? We tip Adama generously.

The rush to board is a mob scene, overwhelming the Malian emigration and customs officials. We elbow our way through and look back at the figure of Adama, who is at the un-ticketed barrier, smiling and waving, shouting something we can't hear. We wave and mount the rolling stairway into the plane. This is how we say good-bye, and it's unlikely we will ever see him again.

Epilogue

We saw no trace of the fighting in the north during our trip, even in Mopti and Djenné. Three weeks after we left Mali, on March 21, 2012, midlevel Army officers deposed the elected civilian government and seized state power. The reason given was that the Malian Army had not been provided with the weapons, support, or training necessary to fight heavily armed Tuareg rebels and their jihadist allies in the north. The Army suffered heavy casualties as a result. The officers alleged that funds earmarked for the military had found their way into the private accounts of government officials.

Meanwhile, the jihadists, many of them foreigners affiliated with Al Qaeda in the Mahgreb (AQIM), brushed aside their one-time Tuareg allies and, by April, had seized control of northern Mali, including Timbuktu. They threatened to capture Mopti, Djenné, Ségou, and Bamako, imposed a harsh form of Sharia law, and massacred Tuareg and Malian soldiers and collaborators. They destroyed Sufi shrines and desecrated Dogon animist ritual sites. Atrocities were committed by all armed factions: the Malian military and militias, the Tuareg, and the jihadists. In January 2013, the French, concerned that a jihadist conquest of Mali would create a militant and aggressive Islamic state run by the AQIM, sent troops, armor, attack helicopters, and jet bombers into Mali, pushing the jihadists out of the cities and villages and into the mountains, where they continue to attack Malian military outposts and civilian communities. Over four hundred thousand Malians have been displaced and are refugees within Mali or in neighboring states.

Tourism in Mali is dead. Karen, Adama's supervisor from the tour agency, remains in Bamako but arranges tours only to Senegal and Burkina Faso. Sophie, the intrepid owner of the hotel in Djenné, is sitting tight despite the proximity of the fighting. There are no tourists to host, but she designs and sells clothes and puts out a monthly blog showing her wares and commenting on the local political scene. Responding to our inquiry, our American travel agent learns from Karen that Adama has had no work as a guide but has survived by doing welding and tile work. We wonder whether his electricity has been connected.

Life has not changed much for people in Mali since we left. The government is still corrupt, and most people are still poor. What is new is the ever-present danger from jihadists and the return of the French colonialists.

The Dogon of the Escarpment have remained in their cliffside villages. They took no part in the fighting and, in fact, gave refuge to Tuareg fighters fleeing the Malian Army and the jihadists. Their heavy dependence on virtually nonexistent tourism threatens their subsistence living. According to Karen, they are now selling their possessions to buy sacks of rice. Their survival is problematic.

In mid-November 2016, Barbara and I visited an art gallery on the upper East Side to see an exhibit of traditional Dogon artifacts. Twenty or thirty pieces were on display and for sale—masks, human figures, and other ritual objects. The dealer in charge of the exhibit told us that during his last visit to the Escarpment in April, he saw only women and children in the villages. The men had all gone to the big cities to try to find work to make up for the loss of tourist income caused by the fighting in the north. He said that the Dogon have sold off all of their traditional ritual objects. This exhibit may contain the last of these treasures.

Iran:

THE ABSENCE OF EVIL

Note: The names of all the people we met in Iran have been changed.

I t starts with Uzbekistan, a possible destination for October 2008.
A friend who has been there thinks we might enjoy its culture,
history, and natural beauty. When we read through a travel guide for
Uzbekistan, however, the most interesting chapter describes a side
trip to Iran. We hadn't seriously thought of traveling to Iran before,
figuring it might be unpleasant, if not dangerous, for American
tourists to wander around a country our government has treated
with such ill will. And then there is the State Department's Travel
Warning: Americans "may be subject to harassment or arrest" and
"should carefully consider the risks" of travel to Iran.

Since the early 1950s, America and its allies have interfered with
Iran's struggle for self-determination. After the fledgling Iranian
Republic nationalized the country's oil production in 1951, the CIA
and British M16 engineered a coup that ousted the democratically
elected government and reinstalled the monarchy in the person of
Shah Reza Pahlavi. The Shah promptly denationalized oil production, and control reverted to American and British corporations.

The Shah ruled as an autocrat for twenty-five years, propped up militarily by the US and supported by his secret police, the Savak. When a popular revolution in 1979 overthrew the monarchy, the Shah fled the country. President Jimmy Carter allowed him to come to the US for medical treatment, and Iranians were outraged. Demanding the extradition of the Shah, students stormed the American Embassy, taking hostages. In retaliation, the US imposed sanctions that crippled Iran's economy.

The American government also supported Saddam Hussein's invasion of Iran in 1980, which was repelled at the cost of more than five hundred thousand Iranian lives, many of them civilians killed by Saddam's use of poison gas.

In his 2008 State of the Union address, President George W. Bush characterized Iran as part of an "Axis of Evil."

Understandably, these actions could generate hostility toward American tourists. Iran's revolutionary leadership doesn't help matters when it refers to the United States as "The Great Satan." However, the pictures of Persepolis, the bridges of Isfahan, the gardens of Shiraz, and the dazzling calligraphic tiles of the great mosques exert a pull. More than that, we are curious about the people. How do they feel about us? About their country?

Our travel agents in Seattle assure us that Iranians differentiate between government policy and individual opinions. They will be happy to see two Americans walking their streets.

During the long flight to Tehran, I read *The Ayatollah Begs to Differ* by Hooman Majd. An Iranian Canadian sits next to me on the plane, glances at my book, and is eager to discuss it. It describes aspects of Iranian culture that affect Iran's domestic and international politics. The culture embraces two apparently contradictory concepts: *ta'arof* (self-effacement) and *haq* (entitlement). An Iranian who invites you into his home for dinner will say at the end of the evening, "Sorry the meal was so poor," or "Sorry we couldn't make things nicer for you." Or, a cab driver may decline to charge you, saying, "It was not worthy." However, you are expected to insist until he relents (and maybe overcharges you). This is *ta'arof*.

On the other hand, when postal workers are notified of a layoff, they go into the streets with drums and banners. Their position is that they are entitled to their jobs regardless of other factors, economic or otherwise. This is *haq*. These concepts, *ta'arof* and *haq*, play out in the diplomatic sphere as well.

The pilot announces that we will enter Iranian air space in a few minutes. There is a flurry of activity as passengers make last call orders for alcoholic drinks and women hurriedly pull scarves over their heads. Barbara reluctantly dons a headscarf, which she wears throughout the trip.

On October 3, 2008, we land in Tehran at three a.m. Amir, our guide, is a cheerful young man who speaks excellent English. Even at that time of day, Tehran's traffic is among the worst we have seen. It is a city of eight million, growing exponentially with a high birth rate and an influx of young adults from the countryside.

One of the first things Iranians will tell a visitor is that they are not Arabs. They are Persians who speak Farsi. Their civilization has developed over several thousand years, and the unspoken implication is that they are culturally superior to the Arabs. They also point out that they practice Shiite Islam, as opposed to the Sunni Islam practiced by most Arabic-speaking peoples. The split between Shiite and Sunni Muslims arose from a dispute over who would lead the caliphate after Mohammed the Prophet's death in 632 AD. Shiites regard Husayn ibn Ali the rightful heir, and Persians and devout Shiite Muslims everywhere celebrate him as a martyr and commemorate his death in battle with a week of mourning, grief, and self-flagellation. On the other hand, the Sunnis believe Yazid, the founder of the Umayyad Dynasty, to be the true caliph. For the outsider, the differences in belief and practice between Shiite and Sunni Muslims are difficult to parse, much less explain. These are issues that even religious scholars argue about. The two factions have been in continuous conflict since the death of the Prophet, and there appears little chance of healing the rift in the near future.

The next morning, we take a walk, as we have many times on many trips. In a park, large groups of women in headscarves and long coats are doing jumping jacks and other exercises, shouting in unison. Barbara waves in solidarity and they wave back.

Near the same park is the Archeological Museum, an impressive introduction to classical Persian culture. It is filled with reliefs and sculptures from ancient cities. One statue in particular, made of carved and polished limestone, catches my eye. Thousands of years ago, an artisan created an archer on horseback, twisted in his saddle, about to release his arrow at his pursuers. It reminds me that Persian civilization goes back to the seventh millennium BC and that, as an Empire, it ruled over the greater part of the civilized world for hundreds of years.

We also visit the famous Carpet Museum, its building shaped like a loom. Many of the carpets are centuries old, with complicated and intricate designs of flowers, animals, Koranic verses, and even hunting scenes. The oldest carpets integrate border illustrations from ancient books. Some have a central medallion, while others present an all-over pattern. The predominant color is a deep red. Also on display are two eccentric carpets, one made for a World's Fair, incorporating portraits of world leaders from Lincoln to the Ottoman Caliph. Another portrays all the Persian kings, each with a number woven into the border, which, like a footnote, references a comment on his reign.

Amir suggests that we not tell people on the street we are Americans, but instead say we're from Canada. We thank him for his concern but decline to take his advice—we want to experience local

Iranians' reaction to citizens of "The Great Satan" and show them that not all Americans share our government's hostility to Iran.

People on the street in Tehran recognize us immediately as tourists with a guide. They smile and try to guess our country of origin, their guess usually being one of the European countries. When they hear we are from the United States, their smile broadens. "Welcome," they say.

We note, also, the young women's minimal compliance with the morality and dress laws. They wear tight jeans, makeup, lipstick, and headscarves the size of a handkerchief. Many have a Band-Aid across the bridge of their nose—a sure sign of a cosmetic nose job. This is particularly the case in north Tehran where the wealthy and well connected live. Iranian women are stunning as they are, and we're sorry to observe that those with money feel the need to emulate western concepts of beauty.

Kerman

Kerman is a city of eight hundred thousand on the southeast plain. There we meet Sadik, our guide and driver for most of the rest of the trip. He is middle-aged, with thinning hair, glasses, an engaging smile, and a sense of the absurd. He prefers to drive his own car rather than depend on someone else. We get the feeling he's not doing this for the money; it seems instead that he enjoys meeting people and showing them his country.

The Friday Mosque is a structure built in 1349 AD during the Safavid dynasty. It is our first direct experience of the magnificent excess of Persian mosques—and we are overwhelmed. The interior and exterior are covered with tiles that display a riot of colors—blue, pink, yellow, beige—and designs featuring flowers, calligraphy, geometric patterns. There are numerous architectural features throughout—arches, stalactites, spiraled columns.

We lunch in a bathhouse that has been converted to a restaurant. A trio of men sing traditional Arab and Persian music, one playing a stringed instrument that he strikes with hammers and the other two on percussion. One of the musicians has the ravaged face and thin body of a heroin addict. In fact, heroin is smuggled over the porous border with Afghanistan, one of the largest producers of opium in the world, and can be obtained in the underground market. This has led to a significant problem with drug addiction in Iran.

The music is sad but compelling, and the songs are mostly about unrequited love. Traditional music from the Middle East has always been one of our favorites, we tell Sadik, to which he replies that his daughter plays the cello for the Tehran Philharmonic, whose repertoire consists mostly of Western classical music.

Sadik is an excellent guide and driver, although he has the disconcerting habit of turning around to talk to us in the backseat while he is driving. I offer to sit in the front passenger seat to avoid the problem and calm our nerves, but Sadik rejects the offer. Either he thinks the front seat is not worthy, in accordance with *ta-arouf*, or that only he is entitled to sit up front, in accordance with *haq*; we can't tell.

On the way to Shiraz, we drive through an unusual landscape—huge rocky outcrops arising out of the desert, devoid of vegetation except for stubby grasses growing in the few patches of soil. Then we descend into a wide valley striped with green orchards of apples, olives, figs, pistachios, pomegranates, and quinoa. Despite some white-knuckle moments when we pass slow gravel-hauling trucks, we arrive safely.

Again, we don't perceive any animosity. At the few checkpoints we encounter, Sadik tells the soldier in charge that we are American tourists, which elicits big smiles and welcomes. When we stop at a gas station to refuel, a man comes over to us and, smiling, hands Barbara a pomegranate.

Shiraz

It is dark by the time we reach Shiraz. Though there are many people out in the bustling street, we are too tired to explore and go straight to bed.

In the morning, Sadik introduces us to our local guide, Fatima, a lovely, charming young woman who wears a headscarf that does little to conceal her long, shining black hair. Sadik teases her for frequently using a Farsi word that sounds like *hup*. Thus sensitized, we begin to hear it everywhere in Iran and then, after we get home, in Iranian movies. No one provides an accurate translation. It seems to serve as a conversation filler, much like our word *so*.

Another conversational quirk: whenever Iranians are unsure about the number of objects, days, people, or other measurements, they resort to the number forty. Sadik tells us that Mohammed had his revelations at age forty, Jesus wandered in the desert for forty days, Ali Baba killed forty thieves, and the mourning period following death is forty days. This is not particularly helpful.

Shiraz is called the city of "roses and nightingales." Fatima leads us through Eram Gardens, a vast park, up and down lanes bordered by cypress, pine, and sour orange trees, with an abundance of alcoves and benches for rest and contemplation. Her youthful energy and enthusiasm contrasts with Sadik's calm, cool demeanor, though they obviously like and respect each other.

Like other mosques we visit in Iran, the Nasir-ol-Molk Mosque is a museum of tiles and architecture. But every mosque is unique. The visual memory we take away from this one is of the light pouring through stained-glass windows onto the lush red carpets, making the interior glow. The exterior is brick, but, as Fatima points out, a select few of the bricks are made of wood to cushion the building in case of earthquakes.

Perhaps the most moving sights in Shiraz are the tombs of the great Persian poets Saadi and Hafez. Both were followers of Sufism, a mystical branch of Islam, whose adherents search for direct personal experience of divine truth and knowledge. Saadi was a widely traveled moralist. His tomb is covered by a turquoise dome and surrounded by a formal garden. Hafez was a lifelong hedonist who wrote

Street poet, Shiraz

of love and wine and never left Iran. He is buried in a copper casket within a polished stone sarcophagus carved with designs and calligraphy, also in a lovely park. Dozens of freshly cut flowers lie on the stones of his tomb, evidence that locals continue to pay their respects. Iranians revere their poetry and poets, including the often-quoted Rumi and Omar Khayyam.

People from all walks of life learn and recite the poems of these masters. Fatima reads one of Hafez's poems to us in Farsi and then in English. A young man, obviously smitten, walks up and engages us in conversation in halting English, but his eyes are for Fatima, who politely but firmly tells him to buzz off.

On a side street near the market, a man sits writing on a tablet. He has a long white flowing beard and mustache. He is writing a poem, and we ask him to read it. The sound and rhythm of the Farsi verses is euphonic. As is often the case, the poem is about love, and, to this poet, about its memory.

Shiraz is a sensory delight. The only trouble with Shiraz is that there is no Shiraz in Shiraz. After the 1979 Revolution, the mullahs pulled out all the grape vines. There is no beer, either. Being caught with alcoholic beverages is a serious criminal offense. Of course, alcohol flows freely at private parties of the wealthy in north Tehran. One day at lunch, we sit in a restaurant a couple of meters from a Dutch tour group that orders beer for the table and is instead served bottles of a near-beer beverage. I won't forget the looks on their faces when they tasted it and then looked at the labels. There was not a second order.

Based on our own taste preferences, the food in restaurants is just okay. Kabobs! Kabobs! Kabobs! Lamb kabobs, beef kabobs, chicken kabobs, fish kabobs—everything except pork kabobs. It is particularly difficult for Barbara, who eats no meat or poultry. Yogurt is her mainstay throughout the trip. However, the Persians do wonders with rice. A dish called *tahdig*, which is generally served at home, is made with rice, saffron, egg, and jeweled bits of fruit, and it has a delicious crust. Tahdig is rarely available in restaurants, and when it is, it's gone in an hour.

Life in Shiraz seems less frenetic than in Tehran. Everywhere, people greet us warmly. They talk to us in the parks and on the street, asking what we think of our president Bush and about where we live (New York City elicits a big "Wow!"). They complain about the morality and dress code police, and I'm surprised at the openness with which they criticize their government. They also go as far as they can to stretch the rules. A street-side restaurant where we eat lunch overlooks a popular spot where young boys and girls in separate cars circle around to ogle one another. Whenever there is a traffic jam or accident, they stop and talk, exchange contact information, or arrange to meet. If they are not interested, they get back into their cars. It's the closest thing we see to a singles bar in Iran.

Persepolis

Persepolis is only a short side trip from Shiraz but a vast journey from the modern Iran we have seen so far. We travel from a young republic striving to have a voice in the Middle East to the remains of ancient Persia, which ruled the civilized world centuries ago. Persepolis was the site of the palaces of the Achaemenid kings Darius,

Xerxes, and Ataxerxes, the first Persian dynasty. The fact that it is very hot and dry has helped to preserve the structures; however, that, plus the absence of shade, has the opposite effect on us. Yet we are caught up in the grandeur of the past and put aside our discomfort. The few other visitors are Iranian.

Stunning bas-reliefs of rulers and noblemen are still intact. There is a twenty-five-meter wall depicting Medes and Persian soldiers (they were allies) leading emissaries of twenty-four different nations by the hand to pay homage to Darius. Huge stone bulls with human heads, bearded in the Persian style, look down impassively. Two-headed griffins open their beaks to snarl.

Carved into the sheer walls of a nearby canyon stand eight enormous Sassanian bas-reliefs showing the victory of Shapur I over the Roman Emperor Valerian in the third century AD. The Sassanian Empire lasted until the arrival of the Arabs in the seventh century.

Firozabad

In a restroom on the way to Firozabad, Barbara encounters eight or nine women washing their feet in the sinks. They stop talking and stare when she enters. They wear full black chadors, but she can see their long pants underneath, in all the colors of the rainbow—a little peek through the window into what the local women wear at home or when they are in exclusively female company. They resume their conversation when she leaves.

In Firozabad, the former capital of the Sassanian Empire, sit the ruins of the winter palace of Ashakur, conqueror of the Parthians, the Romans, and just about everybody else at the time (224–241 AD). We climb a steep cliff to a fortress that overlooks the river and the road. It was built as a final stronghold for the Emperor and his family in case of overwhelming attack. The view is awesome, a dramatic landscape of great shelves of stone rising tilted out of the flat, arid plain. Here, with a sigh of relief, Fatima yanks off her headscarf and her hair tumbles out. She says we can't be seen up here. Fatima is single and would like to get married, but she believes men are intimidated because she owns a travel agency and is self-supporting. Docile wives are usually preferred, but she's not about to give up her independence.

On the road back to Shiraz, we stop to talk to a shepherd with his flock. He and his wife are nomads, owning 120 sheep and goats, a few chickens, a crippled dog, and a tiny tent. Life has been especially difficult due to the past two years of drought.

Dinner is in the town of Yord in a faux nomadic tent with pillowed platforms and a three-piece ensemble playing traditional music. We are surrounded by Iranians, who are all having a good time. Later, we join "forty" Shirazians on the long line for ice cream from Baba's. I keep thinking about the nomad couple on that windswept plain. There was nothing faux about their accommodations.

Yazd

On the way from Shiraz to Yazd, there sits a one-hundred-year-old ice house, still in use. It is a seventy-foot cone-shaped structure of thick-walled masonry encircled by a spiral ledge. It looks like an enormous Dairy Queen, more graceful and energy-efficient than a modern freezer.

Yazd's fortified walls were the last refuge of Iran's Zoroastrian community after the arrival of the Arabs. There are two Zoroastrian "Towers of Silence" where, up to fifty years ago, the remains of the dead were carried and allowed to decompose and be eaten by birds before burial of the bones. There is also a Zoroastrian fire temple, where a fire has been burning continuously since 470 AD.

Zoroastrianism is the world's oldest monotheistic religion. Zoroastrians believe that active participation in life

One-hundred-year-old ice house near Abarkuh, Yazd Province

through good deeds and truth telling leads to a peaceful after-life. Fire and water are considered conduits of wisdom and life-sustaining purity. Prayers to the Creator are offered in the presence of fire. It was the official religion in Persia until the Arab conquest, after which it was suppressed. There remain an estimated 2.6 million Zoroastrians in Iran and India.

The streets are crowded after dark, people meeting and greeting one another in the mild weather. We negotiate the warren of old town streets and alleys to emerge at the central square. A facade serves as a platform for viewing the parade of flagellants during the week commemorating the death of Husayn ibn Ali. It is backlit at night, a dramatic reminder of his sacrifice for the faith.

As we stroll around, four young men in military uniform approach. I immediately think, *What have we done wrong?* But they are smiling. One of them, who speaks English, asks where we are

Soldiers, Yazd

from, and they are all delighted when I answer, "The United States, New York City." They want to talk politics, and their first question is: "What do you think of our President, Ahmadinejad?" (At the time, the US and Iran were at loggerheads over Iran's processing of fissionable material that could be used in a nuclear weapon. Iran maintained it was only for use as fuel to generate energy.) I reply that I disagree with him on a number of social issues but support his position that Iran has a right to develop its own energy sources, especially under conditions of a boycott imposed by America and its allies. The soldiers ask questions about America, New York, and our travels. They cheerfully pose for pictures with me, and we shake hands.

Propped on a table next to the bed in our hotel room is a small American flag.

Isfahan

Like Shiraz, Isfahan is a beautiful city with many parks and boulevards, as well as three magnificent bridges spanning the Zeyandeh

River. The heart of the city is Imam Square, the world's second largest public square (Tiananmen Square in Beijing is the largest). It was once a polo field where matches were played for the amusement of royalty but is now a green space for the public to enjoy. Two sides of the Square are lined with workshops of craftsmasters. Silversmiths, coppersmiths, miniaturists, textile purveyors, carpet salesmen, woodwork and inlay artisans, tile crafters, and makers of the local sweet nougat ply their trades.

Visiting the workshops, we are attracted by the artistry of the miniatures. The artisan spends a lot of time explaining the techniques of his craft. We select a piece of a young woman supporting her drunken elder, and the bargaining begins. He names a price and we counter. He then says, "Pay whatever you think the work is worth." This, of course, creates a dilemma: too low a price is an insult, and too high a price is extravagant. We name a figure, and he instantly agrees—we have been outmaneuvered. As lawyers, we know how to negotiate, but he has taught us a lesson. This was an exercise in *ta'arof*.

Two beautiful domes dominate the square. The dome of the Royal Family Mosque has a turquoise background and an arabesque black-and-yellow pattern. The dome of the Mosque of the Sheikh Lotfollah has a cream-colored background with blue flowers and calligraphy.

The interiors of these mosques are even more stunning architecturally and aesthetically. Calligraphic glazed tiles are set against a stucco background, creating a play of light as we move through the domed prayer room. Blues dominate, deep-blue with white flowers in the *mezrab* (prayer niche) and light-blue honeycomb squinches (dome supports) in each upper corner. Dark corridors open into chambers full of light, color, and soaring columns with shining stylized verses from the Koran. There are no sculptures, portraits, or representational paintings—just pure color and design to induce peace and encourage virtue in the faithful.

Our first morning in Isfahan, we walk along the river. Migrating cranes stand in the shallows. A fog on the river disperses early under the Persian sun. The water level is low due to the drought.

Isfahan's bridges are her jeweled necklaces, and the most beautiful is the Kajou, built in 1650 AD, at the height of Persian achievements in art and architecture. It has two arched levels along its length with a covered pavilion in the center. Lighted at night, it is a magnet for strolling couples and a meeting place for friends. During the day, it shelters singers, artists, and whoever seeks shade and tranquility.

Crossing the bridge, we are drawn to the sound of rich male voices and stop to listen. A group of eight older men sit in an archway, singing a cappella songs based on the poetry of Hafez. Their voices are strong, the acoustics excellent. "These men are retired and they meet here every day to socialize and sing," Sadik says.

We come across a more somber scene—a cemetery with the graves of twenty-three thousand martyrs of the eight-year Iraq–Iran

Local cemetery of martyrs of the Iraq–Iran War, Isfahan

war. Each grave has a small Iranian flag and a photograph of the young man who died, his life barely begun. These are just the dead from the Isfahan district. The cemetery is quiet. It's been twenty years since the War ended, but fresh flowers still decorate some of the graves.

Our hotel is a former Ottoman residence with rooms surrounding a lovely courtyard, where we have dinner. We invite a member of the staff, who is sitting nearby and watching us eat, to our table. He declines with a smile but continues to hang around even though he can't understand a word of what we say. He speaks to Sadik, who translates, "He says he likes you better than any other guests he has met here."

Abyaneh

Abyaneh is one of the oldest towns in Iran. The town is sprinkled with visitors from Tehran and Isfahan, who come to view the quaint houses, streets, and traditional dress still worn by the locals. The women wear full black skirts, white headscarves with bright pink flowers, and long blouses with different floral patterns. The men wear loose black pants with flared, wide legs.

The houses are similar to those of Ottoman cities in the nineteenth century—two floors and a roofed balcony that hangs over the street from the second floor. As in many villages, the entrances have two doors, side by side, one for men and one for women, distinguished by brass doorknockers of different designs. Adobe stairways and paths run uphill from the main street.

Charming as the village is, we sense that something is missing. A great number of the houses are empty, and we see no young people. They have left the town to get jobs in the cities, sending remittances but not returning. This is a plight typical of rural Iran.

The villagers and the visitors we encounter are friendly. Townspeople offer us fruit leather and patiently pose for photos. A family from Isfahan takes pictures of the most exotic thing they have found in this old town—us.

Tabriz

We fly to Tabriz, in the far north of Iran. Our guide is a modest and unassuming young man in his thirties. Later, while we are eating lunch, people come to our table in a steady stream to shake his hand and take pictures, to which he submits good-naturedly, not minding the interruption. It is only then that we learn he is the host of a very popular children's show on television.

Because of its proximity to the border with Armenia, there are more churches in Tabriz than in other parts of Iran. Discrimination by the Shah stoked rebellion in this area before it broke out in the rest of the country. Today, two seats each are reserved in the national parliament for representatives of the Christian, Jewish, and Zoroastrian faiths.

We visit a magnificent bazaar, so huge we feel we will never emerge. The vendors and products are of Armenian origin. These shopkeepers are masters at selling and bargaining, but we manage to resist.

In the mountains north of Tabriz, near the Turkish and Armenian borders, sits St. Thaddeus the Martyr Armenian Cathedral, a structure dating back to 66 AD. It has been destroyed by earthquakes three times and rebuilt, and it is now empty. The village that once surrounded it is gone. Russian troops looted it during World War II, and one of its famous vast carpets somehow wound up in the British Museum. Armenians make an annual pilgrimage to this site, though fewer and fewer make the trip each year.

I take a walk to view the mountain range north of the cathedral and recognize one of the peaks. A check of my map confirms my hunch—it is Mount Ararat of biblical fame. Mount Ararat is technically in eastern Turkey, where I've seen it before. It is a nearly perfect symmetrical massif, its summit covered with snow. It was here before any of the dynasties, empires, palaces, and fortresses and will be here when and if the waters rise again.

Owner and cashier at a restaurant in the carpet bazaar, Tabriz

We return to Tehran, take a last walk in the park near the hotel, and get ready for our early-morning departure. About an hour into the long flight home, the pilot announces that we have left Iranian airspace. A cheer goes up, the scarves come off, and the rolling bar does a brisk business.

Epilogue

We did not ask the Iranian people we met how they felt about their government because we didn't want to make them uncomfortable or put them in any danger. However, some—more than we expected— raised the issue on their own, criticizing President Ahmadinejad and hoping that he would be defeated in the upcoming elections in June 2009. Ahmadinejad was indeed reelected, but allegations of voting irregularities sparked large and widespread street protests, which were eventually put down by the government.

In 2013, Hassan Rouhani was elected president, and although ultimate control remains in the hands of the Supreme Leader and the Mullahs, he took tentative steps to improve relations with the international community.

In 2015, the United States and other countries reached an agreement with Iran whereby Iran would allow inspection of its nuclear facilities in exchange for subsequent relaxation of sanctions on the Iranian economy.

Iranians are deeply committed to their country. They regard themselves as the heirs and guardians of an ancient culture of beauty and creativity. They are concerned about the distorted image Western media has projected on them. They do not seek war. However, twenty-three thousand graveyard pictures of young men in Isfahan tell me how tough and determined they would be in any conflict. They want the right to determine their legitimate place in the region and the world without outside interference. They want respect. That is their *haq*.

The Orinoco, Venezuela:

IN HUMBOLDT'S WAKE

All of the names in this narrative have been changed.

It is November 2015. Having survived a bumpy ninety-minute flight from San Carlos, Venezuela, we land at the airport in Puerto Ayacucho. This is a return leg of an Orinoco River journey we had taken during the previous two weeks. The plane is a four-seater, single-engine Cessna. Barbara and I sit in the two back seats, mine behind the pilot. Our guide, Rodrigo, is in the front passenger seat. A fourth passenger wearing a government identity tag, who boarded at the last minute, sits on a hastily added seat next to the luggage in the rear.

Throughout the flight, the pilot texts on two cell phones simultaneously and lets go of the controls for minutes at a time. This makes Barbara very nervous. When we finally land at the small terminal for private planes, we say, "Bravo!" to the pilot, but he puts his finger to his lips.

As we disembark, we are suddenly surrounded by eighteen Venezuelan National Police, heavily armed, in dark-gray fatigues and black boots. They order us to stand away from the plane. They remove all luggage and cargo and search every bag, going through socks, underwear, Dopp Kits, medication, wallets—everything. They collect our passports. A package is pulled out of the pilot's gear, laid on the tarmac, and sliced open, revealing a slab of raw bacon.

A female officer searches Barbara's bag while a male officer looks through mine. It later strikes us as ironic that they would extend us this courtesy while restricting our movements. Nothing untoward is found in our packs. Our clothes are neatly refolded and everything, including our passports, returned to its rightful place. We are not permitted to touch the baggage.

In addition to all the bags and contents strewn on the tarmac, Barbara notices a large plastic shopping bag stuffed with paper currency. She cannot tell whether the bills are Venezuelan or American. In this case, it makes a huge difference—the value of the contents in US dollars on the black market would be more than five hundred times its worth in Venezuelan bolívar.

The National Police chief, the pilot, and the fourth passenger engage in heated conversation in rapid Spanish, which we can't understand. Suddenly, our baggage is reloaded, and we are ordered to get back in the plane, joined by Rodrigo, the pilot, and a police officer. The fourth passenger is led off by National Police. We never see him again.

We taxi to the main terminal, where our bags again go through careful scrutiny by security. We are separated from our passports for what seems like an unduly long time. A woman is pointing out our numerous immigration stamps to other personnel. At this point, we are concerned, but not yet alarmed.

Rodrigo is taken away to a room for interrogation. Are we next? It would be easy enough for the *Commandante* to say, "Take them all in. We'll sort them out later." I can imagine the warm reception our complaint to the American Embassy will get, given the State Department's repeated warnings about criminal activity in Venezuela.

Rodrigo later tells us that he was strip-searched and was frightened and humiliated. He reports that there were, in fact, two bags of currency—apparently one bag with dollars and the other with bolívar. Rodrigo believes that the trip to the main terminal was to make everything seem normal so as to entrap the intended recipient(s) of the funds. The ruse seems to fail as nobody comes forward to claim the bags.

How did we wind up in this situation?

In 2014, we watched a documentary about the Yanomami, a people living deep in the Brazilian and Venezuelan rain forest. The fierce and independent Yanomami are fighting to protect their territory and traditional way of life against incursion by the West. We would like to see this indigenous culture while it is still relatively intact.

The Yanomami live in isolated groups. Access to their villages is strictly limited in Brazil because of abuses perpetrated by Brazilian and foreign mining and ranching interests, as well as the vulnerability of the people to illnesses to which they have not yet developed immunity. Venezuela allows contact with the villages, but only if the Yanomami agree. They have been known to react with violence to unwelcome visitors.

The recent publication of *The Invention of Nature: The World of Alexander Von Humboldt* by Andrea Wulf reinforces our curiosity. Humboldt, a Prussian, was considered the greatest natural scientist of the mid-nineteenth century. One of his earliest explorations was of the Orinoco River and its tributaries. He met with indigenous people and was the first to map the area. Humboldt kept a meticulous journal. It would be exciting to follow in his wake, stop where he stopped, see what he saw, and sleep where he slept.

We are also interested in the current political situation in the country. Since the election of Hugo Chávez in 1999, Venezuela has had a socialist government, vilified by the American government and press. Chávez focused on improving life for the poor through better housing and free education and medical care. He died in 2013, and with the worldwide plunge in the price of crude oil and the widespread corruption in the current government, the situation has deteriorated. Parliamentary elections are scheduled for December 6, 2015. We want to see what's happening on several levels: Does any part of Chávez's legacy remain? Are the shortages and long lines reported in our media true? How are the people and government preparing for elections?

It is April 2015, and the tide of circumstance is running against our hope to visit Venezuela and travel up the Orinoco River in November. One thing after another casts a shadow on our prospects, the darkest that of my heart surgery in June 2015. The operation (repair of a leaky mitral valve) is minimally invasive (they don't have to crack the sternum). However, at age seventy-seven, one does not heal quickly. I am well enough by September to say yes to the trip, with the concurrence of my cardiologist. But I still worry about floating around in the rain forest with a game ticker, hundreds of miles from professional help.

Further, the distressing reports about the situation in Venezuela increase. Not only is the economy in shambles and the political leadership incompetent and undemocratic, the crime rate in Caracas has soared, the currency is virtually worthless, and Venezuela is at swords' points with its neighbors Colombia and Guyana, each accusing the other of abducting civilians, protecting terrorists, smuggling, sheltering drug cartels, and fostering production of cocaine, to say nothing of disputes over territorial rights.

Yet, once again, our curiosity outweighs the risk. So off we go.

The plan is to explore the delta of the Orinoco in northeast Venezuela, then proceed by boat to travel the upper Orinoco and its tributaries, camping on the way, and, if possible, to visit a Yanomami village before returning to Caracas and flying home.

To begin our exploration of the delta, we fly to Puerto Ordaz where we are met by Nina Ruffenach, who, with her husband Roger, runs the Oridelta Camp, the base for our excursions. Driving down the two-lane road to the Camp, we come upon a strange scene. The road is blocked in both directions by a barricade of logs, large stones, scrap wood, and other heavy objects. People from the nearby town of Susamo have constructed the blockade to force the government to provide tanker trucks of fresh water that had been promised weeks before but were never delivered.

Traffic begins to back up on both sides of the barricade. The villagers are out in force, explaining to frustrated drivers why they had to resort to such means. Drivers and passengers, including Nina, begin calling their political contacts on their cell phones. Soon everybody is sitting or standing around, talking and laughing. When a dump truck seems about to push its way through the blockade, the villagers rush to get in the way and the truck stops.

Within two hours, a water-tanker truck appears. The driver confers with the villagers, presumably regarding future deliveries. Then a cheer goes up, the barricade goes down, and the water is delivered. This is our first experience with the chaotic state of affairs in the government—and with the courage and ingenuity of the people.

The Ruffenachs are genial, conscientious hosts. Nina, who speaks only Spanish and German, her native tongue, is delighted to find that Barbara can also speak German. The setting is beautiful, the food good, and the rooms simple and comfortable. But there are no other guests, and Nina and Roger don't mention future bookings.

The Orinoco Delta consists of many deep channels leading from the river to the Caribbean Sea. Our four days in the area are spent in greater part in an open outboard motor boat, racing through

Blockade on the road to Piacoa

channels, skirting the islands, and spooking flocks of white egrets, blue herons, and Technicolor macaws.

One of the channels is a favorite feeding spot for the Orinoco River dolphin. Roger steers the boat around and around in thirty-meter circles. The dolphins, investigating the noise, begin to leap out of the water. Two meters long, they arc above the surface, affording a good look at their sleek bodies and piebald black-and-white markings. A small sardine, pearly scales glistening, jumps into our boat, fleeing the dolphins. "Should we throw it back?" I ask. "No," Roger says, "I'll give it to my cats."

The tide is low when we reach the Caribbean. An undulating beach of tidal pools and gray sand stretches to the horizon. I'm eager to get in the water. As I swim in the nearby channel, I observe Roger, his pant legs rolled up, beating the water with a stick.

"What are you doing?" I ask.

"At high tide, sting rays bury themselves in the stream bottom," he replies. "They leave their burrows as the tide ebbs. However, sometimes one will remain, and splashing with the stick should flush it out."

I cut my swim short.

When I dry off, I see outlines in the sand where these lethal beauties had buried themselves at high tide. The imprints are enormous, about one meter across, with a one-meter tail tipped with a barb that could kill you. Not a great place to go wading.

There are two Warao families living near the beach in bamboo huts with thatched roofs. Naked children scramble up and down ladders, giggling. One hut is a platform raised on stilts with thatching and sheltering eaves. The other, closer to the beach, is little more than a shed at ground level. Both have smoldering fires under bamboo grills, smoking dozens of dressed fish. These families are completely isolated. There is no school for their children. They live off the grid.

The equatorial sun beats down like a hammer, and the occasional brief but torrential rain leaves us soaked. We cover our New York pallor with long sleeves and trousers and use plenty of sun-screen, but we get burned, anyway. Yet, we can't complain. This is a riverain culture where people travel in boats, and the breeze is refreshing when we cruise at full throttle. The towering sunsets over the delta display colors throughout the red spectrum, from pink to tangerine.

We dock at an inn in the town of San Francisco de Guayo, where, a century ago, Capuchin monks established a school for the local Warao villagers. The school is still functioning. A resident nun greets us and shows us her "museum," a room where she keeps crafts made by indigenous women. The pieces, carvings, basketry, toys, and woven hammocks are of the highest quality, the latter being prized throughout Venezuela. The electricity in the room is off, and the good Sister keeps up a rapid monologue while waving her flashlight.

We buy two baskets, hardly able to see them because of the erratic source of illumination, but we are not disappointed. The hammocks are too bulky for us to take home. I try one out at the inn and have no trouble falling asleep.

The school is well maintained, but an adjacent Chavista housing development is clearly neglected, with front doors and shutters hanging off their hinges and floorboards missing. Money for repairs is simply not available.

We fly back to Caracas and on to Puerto Ayacucho, where Rodrigo, our guide and interpreter for the trip up the Orinoco, and Señor Hermoso, the local trip organizer, are waiting. They take us to a fishing supply store to buy some hooks and line as gifts for the Yanomami. The town is covered with posters and draped with banners of political parties seeking votes in the upcoming election. The government's advertisements predominate. But there are long queues for such things as cleaning supplies, toilet paper, diapers, sanitary pads, cooking oil, and other necessities. Cash withdrawals from banks are limited to one day per week per person, with a maximum of thirty thousand bolívar (about fifty-four US dollars). These hardships speak louder than the posters.

Rodrigo is a young student from Merida, a university town in the Andean foothills. He works in a bookstore, teaches French, and freelances as a guide and interpreter—three jobs to barely make ends meet.

Señor Hermoso invites us to his home for a beer. His house is substantial and comfortably furnished with modern furniture and many appliances. He is a tall, portly man in his fifties who bustles his way through his business day, usually on the phone in his SUV.

The next day, the four of us drive to the port on the Orinoco where our boat is moored. The boat is about fifteen meters long and two meters wide, with a canopy that shelters half its length and provides an upper deck on which to tie down supplies and baggage.

There is space for a makeshift kitchen and hooks for hanging hammocks to sleep or relax. The unsheltered front of the boat is filled with standing barrels of gasoline and motor oil.

There is a crew of two—León, the nominal captain, and Victor, the pilot. Neither speaks English. Rodrigo will share crew duties and translate for us. León is a lanky, garrulous man. I never see him in anything but surfer shorts and a T-shirt. He is also the cook. His breakfast *arepas*, cheese or meat in a pocket of fried dough, are outstanding, as is his tomato, onion, and red bean sauce for pasta.

León's other job is to deal with the numerous National Guard checkpoints along the Orinoco—no small task. All commercial craft have to put in and submit to examination of passports, identification, and, at the discretion of the local commander, a search of the boat. This is purportedly to prevent smuggling of drugs, gasoline, and motor oil. Much of the Orinoco constitutes the border with Colombia, where cheap Venezuelan gas and oil can be sold at great profit.

In reality, these checkpoints are tollbooths for the National Guard Commanders. León negotiates a "donation" of gasoline or motor oil, which is siphoned by Guardsmen from our barrels into their jerry cans. They let us pass. At several checkpoints, we watch the jerry cans being loaded into a motorboat and sent on their way to Colombia. I question Rodrigo about our fuel supply.

"Not to worry," he says, "We always plan ahead to make sure we have enough extra for the tolls. In Venezuela, we don't have enough clean water, but we can take a shower in oil."

Victor, the pilot, is the Mark Twain of the Orinoco. He has lived on the river all his life. He knows nearly everyone and, more important, every sandbar, snag, and shoal in the river. This knowledge is critical, because we are in the dry season and the water is low. Victor is short and very strong. Whenever we look at him, he is smiling.

Like the Mississippi, the Orinoco is an opaque caramel color. Unlike the Mississippi, it is not yet heavily polluted. Where the

Orinoco meets one of its blackwater tributaries, a clear line appears on the surface of the water with caffe latte on one side and black tea on the other. The Orinoco is warm. The tributary is cold.

We follow Humboldt's route from the Orinoco to the Autana River. The land is wild and unspoiled. Peaks called *cerros* rise three to four hundred meters, straight up from the green sea of the rain forest canopy. The cerros have nearly flat tops with dark red corrugated sides that turn blood orange in the sunset. They are volcanic plugs, eons old, the cooled molten lava that remained standing as the surrounding land eroded away. Lava rock lies everywhere, from school bus–sized boulders thrown thousands of feet by the exploding volcanoes to undulating acres of rough black lava stone, marking the path of the fiery flow after the eruption. Upstream, lava stone constricts the river, resulting in stretches of white-water rapids, the passage sometimes narrowing to a funnel or chute, the river then a monstrous fire hose, spume roaring through a stone window.

Cerro Autana

Throughout our journey, pristine sandy beaches provide places to eat, swim, or camp. Meals consist of plantains, pasta, vegetables, and occasionally freshly caught fish. We sleep in a tent on cots that are rigged with their own mosquito netting. This foils the mosquitoes but not the *puri-puri*, a minuscule insect that burrows through the netting and inflicts a tiny bite that looks like a pencil marking. By the end of the trip, I can connect enough dots on my legs and feet to form a dragon tattoo. Fortunately, the puri-puri are not malarial.

In his diaries, Humboldt described a place on a bend of the river, with a view of Cerro Autana. His description and his sketches match that of one of our campsites. The river slows as it turns and forms a clear, cold pool that we quickly take advantage of to cool off, wash up, and swim. Several families live in this paradisiacal setting. They maintain a thatched-roof, open-sided shelter for visitors to sleep under, and we set up our cots and hammocks in this breezy shed. We share our dinner with the resident families.

A boy in his early teens, Lewis, somewhat limited socially, takes a shine to Barbara and me. He speaks little Spanish and no English. He follows us around, polite and deferential. Despite his limitations, he figures out how to set up our mosquito netting, something we and Rodrigo are struggling to do. He also gives us a figure of a bird and other objects he has constructed from palm leaves, complicated pieces that resemble origami. Just before dinner, with the whole crowd at one big table, Lewis brings us *coronas* (crowns), also cleverly fashioned from palm leaf. We wear them that night and the next morning, when we say good-bye.

We return to the Orinoco to search for the Yanomami. León has heard that there is a large Yanomami village named Meri off the Casiquiare River. Somewhere along our route is the path leading from the river to the village. León hopes he can find someone who knows where that path is. The Casiquiare, which connects the

Orinoco and Amazon basins, was first mapped by Humboldt. This river is unusual in that its current reverses direction depending on the timing of heavy rains in each basin.

We settle into a long boat ride with few stops. The Casiquiare is broad, most of the time in excess of a kilometer. The view never changes—an obsidian expanse of water with a border of intense green, above which cottony clouds build slowly into iron-gray thunderheads. Victor sometimes swings close to shore to avoid midstream shallows, and we get a better look at the forest. We see plenty of flora but no fauna—no thirsty jaguars, sweaty tapirs, or toothy caimans. The hours crawl by and the ride becomes exhausting. It rains every day, sometimes in torrents.

Despite drinking vast quantities of water, I suffer a couple of bouts of dizziness brought on by dehydration. Fortunately, both spells occur while we are moored, waiting for the National Guard to finish siphoning our gasoline, and I'm able to get a quick saline IV at the local clinics—for free. One clinic is staffed by a Cuban doctor who is spending two years in Venezuela in connection with a program sponsored by the Cuban government. He is eager to practice his English and sits with us for an hour while the saline drips. He is delighted that we have visited Cuba.

Although the clinic has supplies for the saline drip, it is short on everything else, the doctor says.

One late afternoon, we come upon a dramatic split rock rising out of the water. It marks Capibara, a small settlement on the riverbank, with a school, soccer field, and power generator.

A young man named Andrew acts as the village "historian." Somehow, Andrew's uncle came into possession of the village, and Andrew is now the only surviving relative willing to live in this isolated spot. He says the community is much diminished from its heyday in the early twentieth century as a German-owned rubber plantation. The foundations of the abandoned home sites can still be found on a bluff

Humboldt's split rock

overlooking the river. There is a graveyard deep in the forest where rubber workers are buried with their possessions. Treasure hunters are attracted by the rumor that the owner of the plantation was buried with gold pieces, though none have yet been found.

According to Andrew, Humboldt, too, had stayed in Capibara, mentioning the split rock in his journal. Andrew shows us a flat king-sized lava stone on which the explorer sat and updated the journal. And so it is—and so do I.

The shelter in which we set up our cots has a door, but no walls.

There are only a few days left to find the Yanomami and spend some time with them. We stop at a sleepy river village, and León goes in search of a guide. He returns alone. Barbara and I are afraid that this path we are seeking does not exist.

At a fork in the river is the nearly deserted resort of Nigal, noted for its dazzling snow-white sand. The place looks like a Soviet gulag in winter. But it is merely a sad collection of guesthouses with no guests. León renews his search for a guide and this time returns with a young Yanomami, Nelson, who lives in Nigal. Nelson, a strapping young man, knows how to get to Meri. He comes aboard and we move on.

After a few kilometers, Nelson waves Victor over to the right bank where there is a short, dilapidated dock and some beached dugout canoes nearly hidden by the overhanging foliage. "This is the path," he says.

We tie up, disembark, and start to walk. Victor stays with the boat. The path is muddy, passing through thick forest for a few hundred meters or so, then emerging into an open area bearing the blackened stubs characteristic of slash-and-burn agriculture. León and Nelson lead the way. We lose sight of them for a while, but they return before we descend into full-blown panic. There is no breeze or shade, and the heat and humidity are suffocating. A solitary old man stands in a barren field as we walk past, smiling and holding a two-meter spear. We wade through streams almost as deep as Barbara's waist and clamber over brush piles that tear at our wet clothes. After an hour, we see what must be the village. It is unlike anything we have ever seen or imagined.

Instead of the usual arrangement of huts around or near a commons, there is a single structure—a stadium-sized oval palisade of bamboo trunks, curved inward to provide sheltering eaves on the inside. The wall encompasses the villagers' living space. There are openings at each end of the oval, one to allow access to the gardens, the scorched fields, and a small stream, and the other for use as an outdoor toilet. Outsiders can neither enter nor leave without the chief's permission. The whole palisade is called a *shabono*. We enter through a small designated opening in the stockade.

The individual family quarters are defined by the three-meter distance between the support posts and, other than for the occasional hanging blanket, are open to the world. The middle of the compound is a common area of about eighty by forty meters. This shabono is three years old, and the villagers are still working to complete it. Eventually the bamboo rots, or the game runs out, and the Yanomami move to a different location and build another shabono.

We find a bustling community. In the commons, bare-breasted women hang wash to dry, and naked children play. Skinny brown dogs make a racket, nip at one another, and whine as the children hit them with sticks. At one end of the common area, women chat and grind manioc to make a flat, crisp bread. Men arrive carrying stringers loaded with fish. Villagers line up to get their share.

About a dozen men sit in the shade beneath the eaves and watch a shaman who sings songs about the forest spirits and mimics their movements with exaggerated gestures, while prancing back and forth in front of his audience. Some of the men wear face paint. They pass around a pipe, smoking *yopo*, an herbal stimulant. The drug clearly has an effect. Laughing, the men shout comments at the shaman. This yopo ceremony was going on when we arrived in midafternoon and continued for two more hours. It takes place every day. Women are excluded.

We wander around, observing the Yanomami at their quotidian tasks, smiling and asking some for photos. A few smiles are returned. They are polite, but we don't feel welcome. For the most part, we are ignored. The Yanomami are not known for their hospitality and, in fact, have a history of resolving disputes with violence, sometimes with fatal results.

Our accommodation is one of the spaces under the eaves, similar to the spaces occupied by Yanomami families. The only amenities are two string hammocks. There is also a homemade smoothbore single-shot rifle and two spears nestled in the overhanging eave. We will be sleeping here tonight. Our toilet is the rest of the rain forest.

Shaman at the yopo ritual, Yanomami village

Yanomami children and a friend

The leadership of the village is shared by two men referred to as the "old chief" and the "young chief." The old chief is an advisor, but the young chief makes the final decisions and sees that they are carried out. The shaman is the repository of the myths and legends that constitute the spirit world of the tribe.

The young chief is in his twenties, short, wiry, olive-skinned, energetic, and given to frowning. Like all the men, he is bare chested and wears loose-fitting shorts. Like some, he wears face paint. He conducts an inspection of the compound and scolds the family who occupies the space next to ours for letting a palm strip binding loosen. He shakes the rifle in the roof to make sure it is secure, all the while ignoring us. The family tightens the binding immediately.

In the fading light of early evening, the men and women of the shabono gather in the commons. The men carry long spears. In a column, by twos and threes, they move forward with little hopping steps. Every few seconds, the men utter a deep guttural cough, like a jaguar makes to freeze its prey. The column stops in front of us, and the men form a semicircle into which the women step, two by two, chanting and dancing. After they finish, we lay out our gifts, the fish hooks and line, which are divided among the men. The young chief brings out a long red cloth and tears one-meter-long pieces from it. He distributes them to the women, who clutch the fabric and hurry to their quarters. They will use the cloth for clothing and decoration. Some women quarrel over perceived unfairness in the distribution, but the young chief speaks sharply to them and they disappear.

Rodrigo and León bring our dinner from the boat. León assures us that the Yanomami will take good care of us and that the crew will return at eight the next morning to pick us up. They wait until the chief gives permission and then leave us alone with the Yanomami.

Evening segues into night. Cooking fires blink around the rim of the oval. Two rooms away, an old man sings softly to himself. Men and women speak in hushed voices. Children laugh and cry. I gingerly mount my hammock and pull down the mosquito netting. The hammock stretches with my weight, enveloping and supporting me, swaying almost imperceptibly, bringing sleep.

But, alas, drinking a lot of water to avoid dehydration results in bladder discomfort that cannot be ignored. It awakens me in the dead of night and will not be put off. I clamber out of the hammock and make for the bamboo gate at the opening in the palisade. I get there but find the gate is tied shut. Desperate, I climb over the gate, scratching my bare legs. I stagger into the field and obtain blessed relief.

On the way back, I am disoriented in the dark. It is impossible to tell one living area from another. I stumble and fall into a family's space, startling its inhabitants. A tall young man arrives, helps me up, and points to my cubicle. I make gestures of apology to the family and return to my hammock.

In the morning, the village slowly awakens. People relax in their hammocks, talking quietly. They stoke their fires and prepare the first meal of the day, often consisting of manioc and other root vegetables.

Eight o'clock comes and goes. No one from the boat appears, but the young chief does. He is not smiling. He gives a curt order to two men, who begin stuffing our possessions into our backpacks. When they finish, he barks a single word in Spanish, "*Vámonos!* (We go!)" And we go—out the little opening in the shabono and into the fields, the Yanomami carrying our gear. Barbara and I are practically running to keep up, not really sure what the young chief plans to do with us. We struggle over the brush piles and splash through the streams, until, finally, we see our comrades coming toward us. Apparently, after sundown, the boat at its mooring was beset by a monstrous cloud of mosquitoes, and the crew had to move down the river to a breezier location.

The young chief and two men come aboard, carrying a defunct outboard motor that he wants to take to Nelson's village to be repaired. I take this opportunity to interview the chief about his job. He is surly but agrees, with Rodrigo translating. His job description includes assigning men and women to hunting, fishing, and construction tasks; inspecting the condition of the shabono's interior and exterior; inspecting rooms, tools, and weapons; heading off violent confrontations among the villagers and mediating disputes; and assuring safe and adequate water supply.

The position is not hereditary. Chiefs are chosen by consensus of the adult males. At this point, he abruptly terminates the interview and goes to sit by himself in the prow of the boat.

On our way to San Carlos, our last stop, we drop off the chief and Nelson at Nigal. Everyone dives into the river for a swim. I express concern about getting to San Carlos in time to get lodging for the night before our flight back to Ayacucho the next morning, but Rodrigo says not to worry. "There will be plenty of options."

There are no options. We sit in the boat, roasting slowly in the afternoon sun while León and Rodrigo try to find shelter. The place is a ghost town, neat rows of houses, almost all empty—another victim of the economic chaos. I have visions of sleeping in the town square under a tree.

Finally, after two hours, Rodrigo returns. "We have a place." I ask if it has a roof. He replies, "It has a roof and is funny."

He is right. It is a former tavern, long since abandoned, on the bluff of the river. The menu is still on the wall, and the place is decked out with pennants, banners, and a mirrored disco ball hanging from the ceiling. Next door is a chicken coop full of chickens, separated from our quarters by thin wire mesh. But we are happy to have the shelter, and we set up our cots and hammocks to the sound of our neighbors' clucking and flapping.

It is four in the morning and dark as death outside. This does not deter the roosters next door from offering their screechy welcome to the coming dawn. Within minutes, everyone is awake, fumbling with pants and shoes, some proposing fried chicken for lunch. León brings breakfast from the boat.

We leave the no-name café and slouch through the deserted dust-blown streets to the airstrip. A civilian wearing a government agency photo ID joins our procession. The next time we see him, he is sitting behind us in the Cessna.

And so, here we are in the terminal in Puerto Ayacucho, without our passports, without a translator, and without a guide, at the disposal of a *Commandante* who must be very angry that things have not gone the way he had planned. But suddenly, a National Policeman hands back our passports and nods toward our backpacks. "Let's get out of here," I say. We head for the door and see Rodrigo waving. He grabs us in an *embrazo* and hustles us over to Señor Hermoso's SUV. We think the Commandante figured we were just dumb gringos who unwittingly provided cover for someone else's scheme. Which may well have been the case.

The next morning, as we are waiting for our flight to Caracas, we have a much more delightful experience in the Puerto Ayacucho airport: in a video promoting tourism, with Cerro Autana in the background, we see Lewis, smiling, holding one of his palm leaf creations.

We spend two days in Caracas with a boundlessly cheerful and enthusiastic Caracan named George who speaks perfect English, loves his city, and drives like a madman, which, in Caracas, is the only way to get anywhere.

The city is beautiful, nestled in the easternmost ridge of the Andes, a few kilometers from the sea. The tonier districts, in particular embassy row, are thick with boulevards, shops, and restaurants.

There are long stretches of streets closed to autos in the old colonial central city, allowing relaxed pedestrian traffic. The heart of the city is Bolívar Square, which features an equestrian statue of the Liberator, as does almost every town square in Venezuela. Simón Bolívar is a virtual deity. He rests in an enormous mausoleum, a sort of secular cathedral, complete with a changing of the honor guard every two hours.

With the elections looming, the square is filled with banner-waving supporters of the various candidates and parties. The largest group is from the government party, the PSUV (United Socialist Party of Venezuela), whose leader is President Nicolás Maduro, Chávez's handpicked successor. Various booths promoting single issues on the environment, spousal abuse, and community organizing line the cobblestoned streets. One booth displays the combined electronic and manual cross-check method of voting used in Venezuela that is designed to keep the vote count honest. Fingerprint and photo identification is required. No hanging chads here. One-on-one debates proliferate, some rancorous, most good-natured. It is raucous democracy in action.

Although Caracas has a (probably well-deserved) reputation as one of the most dangerous cities in the world, no one harasses or otherwise bothers us in any way as we wander the streets. But the beauty of the setting and the grandeur of the wealthy areas cannot hide the favelas with makeshift houses lining the hills above the city center, a symbol of the poverty that still pervades the country despite its abundant natural resources.

Moreover, corruption permeates the social order, especially in the government. The trappings of an economy of scarcity, such as long queues for basic needs, hang incongruously on the beautiful capital of a country sitting on what is perhaps the world's largest oil reserves.

The Chavistas claim corruption and scarcity is, in large part, caused by domestic and foreign oligarchs taking billions of dollars out of the country, by Saudi Arabia artificially holding down the price of petroleum, and by US funding of far-right parties that have engaged in violent street demonstrations. They claim the goal of the opposition is to undo all the social programs Chávez initiated—free schooling, free medical care, universal electrification, literacy, affordable housing—programs critical for a decent quality of life in the favelas and poor villages of Venezuela.

All of which is probably true.

The opposition claims that the social programs were unrealistically premised on the price of oil remaining above one hundred dollars per barrel. They state that the government's monetary policy is absurd, that public monies are being siphoned off by corrupt officials, that the social programs are blatant unaffordable pork barrel, and that the government is using intimidation to silence criticism and dissent.

All of which is probably true.

It doesn't help the Chavistas that, compared to Chávez, Nicholas Maduro has the charisma of a brick wall.

We drive up into the foothills where the American embassy compound is located, and park at an overlook above the grounds. The facility is vast, taking up a few hundred acres of the side of a mountain. It includes an exclusive golf course. Most of the nearby residents are embassy employees. If nothing else, the size of the diplomatic facility and the presence of hundreds of employees indicate more than a passing interest in Venezuelan affairs. And given the long and sordid history of US covert and overt interference in the affairs of Latin American countries, there is little reason to assume it is not occurring in Venezuela.

Back home in New York, friends and family ask about our Orinoco trip. "How was it?" We decide to use a one-word reply that is sufficiently descriptive and ambiguous: "Memorable."

Epilogue

Summer 2016. Venezuela is in crisis.

After the opposition won almost two-thirds of the seats in the National Assembly in the December 2015 elections, the situation rapidly deteriorated. President Maduro dug in his heels, protecting his cronies and continuing disastrous policies.

As a result, public hospitals lack supplies, working equipment, and life-saving medicines. There are water shortages and electrical outages throughout the country. There is a long wait to purchase scarce basic goods. Inflation is rampant. The price of crude oil, on which the economy depends, continues to fall. The Venezuelan currency, the bolívar, is virtually worthless.

Government employees work only two days a week, and the political system has come to a standstill. The government has declared a state of emergency, but nothing is getting done due to the conflict between the opposition and the president. They cannot even agree about whether to accept foreign aid to help them through the crisis. The opposition itself is fractured.

On September 2, 2016, hundreds of thousands of Venezuelans converge on the capitol, Caracas, to demonstrate their opposition to the government and call for a referendum that, if successful, would force an early election for the presidency. The government organizes counterdemonstrations, accusing the opposition of planning a coup and using violence against government supporters. Maduro refuses to resign. The economic crisis deepens.

Stunned and saddened by these developments, we think about the generous, kind people we met in 2015 and wonder how they are surviving in a society about to collapse. For a few weeks after our return to Brooklyn, we communicate with Rodrigo. However, since the elections, our emails go unanswered.

Meanwhile, in response to our complaint about being implicated in suspect activity at the Ayacucho airport, the director of the local travel agency initially claims that the "mystery passenger" was merely carrying money from remote villages to be deposited in the banks in Puerto Ayacucho. He apologizes profusely for our inconvenience.

Later, however, he states that the stranger was a "duly identified official in charge of the elections" to whom the pilot was obliged to offer "urgent service." No one was authorized to examine his baggage. Allegedly, the official had waited for military transport, but none was available.

But all of us had seen an enormous military transport plane on the tarmac in San Carlos taking on passengers while the mystery man stood around. And no one has explained why eighteen National Police were waiting in Puerto Ayacucho to surround and search our plane and our luggage and strip-search our guide.

We think we were caught in a minor episode of "business as usual" in Venezuela. We will probably never know the whole story.

State of Palestine

The terms Israel and Israeli in this narrative refer to the Government of Israel and/or the Command of the Israeli Defense Force (IDF). Many in Israel, both Jewish and Arabic, actively oppose the militarist policies of their government, the occupation of Palestinian land, and the violation of Palestinian civil and human rights.

Prologue

In April 2009, we hear from a friend that Code Pink, a women-led antiwar organization founded to protest the Iraq War, is organizing a delegation to Gaza at the invitation of the United Nations Relief and Works Agency (UNRWA).

We have been active in antiwar, civil rights, and social justice issues, including Palestinian causes, and have traveled extensively in the Middle East. Barbara and I decide to join the delegation.

The Gaza Strip is a narrow piece of land bordering the eastern Mediterranean Sea. It is twenty-five miles long and approximately three to seven miles wide, with a population of 1.5 million in 2009. A larger number of Palestinians live in the West Bank, a landlocked territory that shares borders with Israel and Jordan. It is generally recognized by the International Court of Justice, the Israeli Supreme Court, the UN General Assembly, and other international bodies that the West Bank is Palestinian territory under military occupation by Israel. The Israeli government deems the West Bank to be a "disputed territory" and has allowed and even encouraged Jewish settlers build communities there in violation of international law.

The day-to-day governance of the Palestinians is divided between two major political parties, Hamas and Fatah. Fatah was founded by and remained closely associated with the revolutionary movement of Yasser Arafat, who died in 2004. In parliamentary elections held in 2006, Hamas, based in Gaza, defeated Fatah, based in the West Bank. Fatah refused to accept the results, and armed elements of the party attempted to oust the Hamas leadership. The coup failed. Fatah retained control of the West Bank. Gaza is governed by Hamas.

There have been discussions about uniting the two parties, but, as of now, the factions are barely on speaking terms.

To the extent that there is any recognition of Palestinian political autonomy, Fatah is supported by Israel and the United States. Despite being the victor in an election certified as fair, Hamas is regarded as a terrorist group. And, ultimate control of both Gaza and the West Bank remains in the hands of Israel.

The Gaza Strip was occupied by Israel until it withdrew in 2005, but in 2007 Israel and Egypt imposed a land, sea, and air blockade, restricting, if not banning, imports of food, medicine, construction materials, and other consumer and industrial goods. With rare exceptions, Gazans are not permitted to cross the border, even to obtain medical treatment or visit their families.

From December 27, 2008, to January 18, 2009, the Israeli Defense Force (IDF) conducted Operation Cast Lead, a continuous air, sea, and land assault on the Gaza Strip. Fourteen hundred Palestinians (mostly civilians) were killed and six thousand injured. The IDF also destroyed most of the civil and industrial infrastructure, as well as large residential areas. The IDF's casualties were thirteen killed, eight by friendly fire.

Why did Israel attack Gaza? The underlying reasons are a matter of speculation and dispute. A cease-fire had been in effect for several months. At some point, the IDF conducted a raid into Gaza to seize an alleged terrorist, and some Gazans retaliated with a few ineffectual rockets. What is not in dispute is that Hamas then offered to reinstate the cease-fire, and the Israeli government's response was to launch Operation Cast Lead.

Amnesty International and Human Rights Watch found massive violations of international law in Israel's conduct of Operation Cast Lead, including, among other breaches: disproportionate violent reaction to minimal provocation; use of banned or partially banned weapons; and deliberate or reckless attacks on civilians and civilian targets, such as schools, hospitals mosques, houses, and ambulances. The blockade has also been deemed to be in violation of international law.

We traveled to Gaza about six months after the end of Operation Cast Lead. Nothing we encountered in our travels (or our lives) prepared us for the devastation we witnessed there. We had seen the pictures and read the reports of the destruction of lives and property. But these do not do justice to the physical and emotional damage we encountered.

The cold numbers do not convey the human story.

Cairo, Egypt

May 28, 2009

The group meets for the first time with the Code Pink leadership at the Pension Roma, a hotel in Cairo. We gather in a small conference room barely able to contain all sixty-six of us, some of whom are squatting on the floor and sitting on the windowsills. Everyone is in good humor, but serious about the mission. We eat meze and fruit and go around the room introducing ourselves. While there is much laughter and badinage, the meeting is well run by Medea Benjamin and Anne Wright, founders of Code Pink. They brief us on logistics and discuss the chances of actually getting into Gaza—about fifty-fifty. We are traveling in two buses, plus an additional truckload of playground equipment. If the Egyptians won't let us cross the border at Rafah, we will camp at the Rafah crossing and set up the play equipment to get the attention of the international press. T-shirts, buttons, and cups are passed around. Then, as often happens during this journey, the group breaks into song.

Cairo, Sinai Desert, Al Arish, Egypt

May 29

We assemble in a downtown parking lot next to two big tour buses. Two carloads of Egyptian Internal Security Officers stand silently nearby, watching us and occasionally murmuring into their cell phones. We mill around for half an hour, waiting for stragglers. Tighe Berry, who calls himself "The Propman," is in charge of the playground equipment. He is everywhere at once, climbing on top of the buses, lashing down the equipment, assuaging nervous bureaucrats on his cell phone, and negotiating with the Internal Security agents. Meanwhile, we sing. Finally, we mount up and move out in a convoy, followed by Internal Security and Tourist Police with AK-47s in pickups and officers in unmarked cars.

Everybody on the trip is interesting. Most are political activists, some are religious pacifists, and others radical leftists. Several are retirees, veterans of antiwar, civil rights, gay rights, feminist, environmental, and other struggles. A number are Jewish. Medea Benjamin has a long history of progressive activism and has worked tirelessly to promote peace efforts and human rights. Ann Wright is a former Lieutenant Colonel in the US Army and former diplomat who resigned because of her opposition to the Iraq war. There are other public figures such as Norman Finkelstein, a professor denied tenure at Hunter College and DePaul University because of his criticism of Israel, and Roane Carey, Managing Editor of *The Nation*. Phil Weiss, creator of the blog *Mondoweiss*, joins us later.

By late afternoon, we arrive at Al Arish, an Egyptian coastal town near the Gazan border. We bed down here, as there are no hotels in Rafah, and will attempt entry tomorrow. A group of us wander through back alleys to get to the beach. Trash swirls in the offshore breeze. Most of the hotels and beach homes are empty, victims of a downturn in tourism. I plunge into the Mediterranean in an uncrowded stretch of beach and discover why it's uncrowded. I'm covered with seaweed; it's like swimming in minestrone. I move down the beach to join crowds of locals cavorting in clearer water.

Rafah, Egypt, and Rafah, Gaza

May 30

In the morning, the buses leave our budget hotel in Al Arish (complimentary cockroaches) for the short trip to the Rafah crossing, accompanied by our armada of uniformed Egyptians. There are two checkpoints to clear. The first is supposed to be the toughest. Denial of entry has been quixotic and arbitrary. Prior delegations have spent days trying, unsuccessfully, to cross the border. An earlier Code Pink delegation waited for two days and was granted entry on the coattails of a British MP.

At the first checkpoint, we wait in the bus. Officers of various rank board and glower at us. They tell us to get off the bus. We get off. Then they tell us to get back on the bus. We get on. Suddenly, they wave us through, truck and all, to the second checkpoint, for baggage and passport check. We cheer and sing. The speculation is that the Egyptians are being nice because Obama is in Cairo and they don't want any embarrassing incidents.

At the second checkpoint, there is a four-hour wait while the Egyptians go through luggage and examine passports. Barbara overhears the passport checkers exclaiming, "Iran, Iran." This could only refer to stamps in our passports, souvenirs of our trip to Iran in 2008. However, nothing comes of it.

Approval is granted by early afternoon. The Egyptians collect our exit fee. We retrieve our passports and luggage, reload the buses, and climb aboard for the final joyful leg of this odyssey—a hundred meters to Gaza. As our buses and truck cross into Rafah, Gaza, dozens of people greet us, cheering, waving, and taking pictures. We cheer and wave back. They usher us into a reception hall where we are warmly welcomed by the Minister of Education. Many security guards are present, this time not watching us but watching out for us. The Minister expresses his concern for our safety from interference by Palestinian extremists and Israeli agents. He urges us to move freely and to talk to anyone, but to stay in groups.

One of the Canadian delegates, who has corresponded via the Internet for eight years with a Palestinian who lives in Gaza, meets him in person for the first time. They announce they are going to be married. Naturally, we cheer and sing.

The United Nations Relief and Works Agency training facility at Khan Yunis is built on the site of a former Israeli settlement. When they left, the Israeli settlers and the IDF destroyed everything—crops, buildings, and all other structures. The land surrounding the UN facility is barren, reclaimed by the desert. A housing project stands half-completed and silent, abandoned for lack of building material.

Much of our time will be spent visiting service facilities funded by the UN and staffed by Gazans. The Agency, though technically restricted to assisting refugees or their descendants (approximately two-thirds of the people living in the Strip), employs or provides some support to 90 percent of the population. Without UNRWA, the economy would collapse.

John Ging, the UNRWA Director, delivers an impassioned plea for help to lift the blockade. He describes it as "arbitrary and deliberately cruel." Only items deemed "essential" by the Israelis are allowed through, and, even those, sparingly. He says that Gazans are unfairly maligned as bloodthirsty terrorists. In fact, they are educated, peace-loving, industrious people who just want to live normal lives like everyone else. Ging fears that Gazans, in particular the young, will lose hope and be recruited by extremists who use illegal violence.

Outside, we mill around buffet tables under an awning shielding us from the sun. The food is good. Of course, there is no alcohol, but the Gazans don't need it to have a good time. Arabic music plays on the PA system, and soon everybody is dancing for the next hour, including the UN support staff, the security guards, the delegates, and the administrators. And me.

Tired and happy about our success at the border, we drive to our hotel in Gaza City, passing several buildings destroyed by IDF planes and gunboats.

Northern Gaza

May 31

The area north of Gaza City, bordering Israel, is dominated by the Jabaliya Refugee Camp. One hundred and fifty thousand Palestinian refugees live in this overcrowded camp. They are among the thousands driven from their homes in Israel and the West Bank in 1948, a mass expulsion known as the *Nakba*.

Remains of a mosque, Northern Gaza

Family's tent in front of wreckage of their house, Beit Hanoun

In a macabre twist, Operation Cast Lead targeted and completely destroyed the American International School, one of the most respected secondary schools in Gaza. The school was a multistory, modern, reinforced concrete structure paid for with US dollars. It now looks like someone stepped on it. Ceilings and floors are pancaked into each other. It was hit by three missiles at night. There was one fatality—a watchman. The night before, he had asked an assistant director whether he could bring his family to stay overnight in the school as they had been terrified by the bombing in their neighborhood. The assistant director declined, saying he could not reach the director to get permission. That night, the watchman died alone while his family stayed home, safe.

The IDF claims the school was used to store munitions. This is vehemently denied by the directors and the staff, and no evidence has been produced to support the claim. Ironically, Palestinian extremists distrusted the school's staff because of its American connection and frequently harassed them. The school lost all of its equipment and books but has since reopened in rented quarters in Gaza City. Only 18 of its 230 students dropped out.

Several hospitals and clinics suffered a similar fate. At the Kamal Edwan Hospital, a new wing had just been built with foreign contributions and was about to open when Operation Cast Lead began. New diagnostic and treatment equipment had been installed and was ready for use. Israeli tanks approached within twenty meters of the hospital and opened fire on the new wing. Shell holes, a meter wide, and shrapnel gouges pockmark the exterior. Every window is blown out. Inside, a doctor takes us on a floor-by-floor tour. Broken glass crunches underfoot. I'm glad I wore heavy shoes. We clamber over twisted metal and slabs of fallen plaster and concrete. Depleted uranium shrapnel litters the floors. Yet doctors continue to treat patients despite the wreckage and a shortage of medicine and supplies.

Kamal Edwan Hospital, Northern Gaza

A collateral benefit to our mission is the chance to meet serious political activists, each with unique stories to tell about their struggles, defeats, and victories. At the hotel that evening, we have a long talk with Rich, a civil engineer with the Coast Guard in Juneau, Alaska, who writes a monthly column for the *Juneau Empire*. He is a quiet, thoughtful guy who seeks the common thread of humanity in everyone. I can imagine the grief he must get on the job for his activism. He is a veteran and has a son with the US Army in Iraq, but he is totally dedicated to the cause of justice for the Palestinians. He is already at his computer sending dispatches when Barbara and I get up for our early morning walk.

Beach Refugee Camp, Gaza

June 1–2

There is not much left of the Government Ministry buildings in Gaza City. They are gutted, hit by land, sea, and air shelling. Tent communities have sprouted where there were once residential blocks. Destroyed mosques and the rubble of entire neighborhoods are everywhere. But there are enough boulevards, beaches, and intact apartment buildings to remind us of what a lovely seaside city this was and could be.

The two major universities in Gaza illustrate the thousand ways the Israeli bombing and blockade make life desperate. Two of the largest buildings at the Islamic University were totally destroyed, and exchange programs with schools in Europe and Egypt have been suspended.

The dean at al-Aqsa University recites a litany of hardships. They cannot obtain books. Faculty cannot go to conferences. They cannot finish construction projects. They cannot visit the West Bank. The dean has a sister in Bethlehem he has not seen in twenty years. He reminds us of Desmond Tutu's admonition: "In situations of oppression one cannot remain neutral. To do so is to side with the oppressor."

Despite all of this, classes go on. Students are educated. People search for some semblance of normality. We talk to several female students who are sitting around the tree-shaded quadrangle of the Islamic University campus. They are giggly and shy but enjoy practicing their English. Although classes were not in session at the time of the attack, two of them were in the university library when they heard the explosions, which, they say, were enormous. They thought they were going to die. Now, we watch them laugh and poke one another.

The modern, well-endowed Qattan Centre for the Child is a model facility, architecturally and functionally. It is funded by an NGO created by a wealthy Palestinian from London. It provides after-school educational services for hundreds of children under age ten and is equipped with a well-stocked and well-used library. The Centre offers computer and art classes, using the latter to treat children with PTSD residual to the Israeli attacks. The government building next door was also attacked, and chunks of shrapnel from the explosions landed on the Centre's roof. Despite the danger, the

Centre's guards refused to leave the premises. We look at the beautiful structure and wonder whether its turn will come next time. Because there always has been a next time.

The director, a woman named Reem Abu Jaber, takes us into a conference room. We drink tea and soda while she speaks of the siege and her own history. The blockade affects every aspect of daily life. It wears people down. It wears her down. "I just want a normal summer," she says. A few years ago, she went on sabbatical, studying the teaching of languages at Wales University but was not happy living in the consumer culture of England. She realized her true happiness lay in helping others. So, she returned to Gaza.

Reem shows us some of the children's paintings. They depict helicopters, bombs, tanks, dead bodies, and bursting white phosphorus shells, with homes and schools in flames. She appears discouraged and tearful, but pulls it together and proudly takes us on a spirited tour of the facility.

The most seriously injured are sent to Al-Shifa Hospital. The director shows us around, his white shirt stained with perspiration. The Israelis allocate only enough electricity to air-condition the operating rooms. It is early June, but the heat in the emergency and waiting rooms is stifling. The power is arbitrarily turned off by the Israelis for periods of four to twenty-four hours, during which time the hospital must depend on diesel-run generators meant to operate for much shorter intervals. Furthermore, fresh fuel for the generators is banned by the blockade, forcing them to use old fuel and endangering the generators, which cannot be replaced.

Patients whose cases cannot be treated at Al-Shifa are taken to the border crossings in hopes of receiving medical attention in Israel or Egypt. According to an Israeli Human Rights group, some patients are told that to be allowed to cross they must collaborate with the IDF or Mossad and name names of militants or political activists. Some who have refused have been denied transfer and have died, and all who have been granted permission to cross are suspected by their neighbors.

Gaza is a traditional male-dominated society, and the high unemployment resulting from the attacks and blockade has caused marital disruption and family stress. A women's center in the Deir al-Balah Refugee Camp provides sanctuary, counseling women regarding issues of spousal abuse, post-traumatic stress disorder, and birth control and abortion. It offers craft and job training and English classes, and there is a flourishing poetry circle where women meet to read and exchange their poems. There is also a computer lab with no power and a gym with no equipment.

We ride the buses to the village of Johr al-Deek, in mid-Gaza on the Eastern border. The village was used as an IDF base. When the IDF pulled out, they dynamited and bulldozed almost all the homes, shelled the school and community center, and destroyed crops, wells, and trees. Two residents were killed, one thousand displaced. The homes were not mud huts, but reinforced concrete structures, some two and three stories, that housed extended families. The larger houses were dynamited and the smaller ones bulldozed. All were demolished except for five houses where the IDF lived during the demolition.

The people of Johr al-Deek are not refugees. They are Bedouin, the original inhabitants of Gaza. The Bedouin are not officially eligible for UN aid, but a few surplus tents are provided. Otherwise, they improvise dwellings with sheets of corrugated metal, carpets, and blankets. Essentially, they live in the rubble of their former homes. Hamas provides food and a few necessities. The mayor conducts the tour. He asks rhetorically, "Why? Why destroy our homes, our livelihood, our wells, our beloved trees?" However, he adds, "We will never leave this place. We will never give up."

Johr al-Deek

People are incredibly happy to see us. They feel alone in a world where no one cares and where they are disposable. UNRWA does all it can, but it's not enough.

More than eleven thousand Palestinian political prisoners are being held in Israel. We meet with some of their families. They hold pictures of fathers, brothers, sons, husbands, wives, sisters, and daughters and tell stories of torture, withheld medical treatment, and denied visitation. One elderly woman, bent over and walking with a cane, has not been allowed to see her son for seven years because the Israelis claim she is a dangerous terrorist. Barbara goes to each of them, takes their hands, and tries to offer words of comfort. Though they thank and bless her, she's frustrated by our inability to help.

That evening, members of International Solidarity Movement (ISM) show us videos they've taken of the harassment of fishermen and farmers. The IDF attacks fishing boats everywhere, even those close to shore. Some of our group who were housed near the beach heard gunfire near dawn on several occasions. It has become impossible for Palestine fishermen to earn a living.

Women's poetry circle at a women's center, Deir al-Balah Refugee Camp

Farmers tending their crops on their land near the border are also regularly fired upon by Israeli border guards. ISM members, with clearly marked orange vests, accompany the farmers in their fields. They carry video cameras and megaphones, announcing their presence. The IDF opens fire anyway. In one recorded episode, a farmer is shot in the leg.

Around ten p.m., a group of us meet with Omar, a Palestinian businessman and intellectual. He was once active in Fatah, the political party that controls the West Bank, but is now disillusioned and speaks at length of the "breakdown of civil society" and how the corrupt bribe-and-kickback-based Fatah/PLO eroded the community service system of Palestinian culture.

Hamas, in contrast, has gained credibility because it provides community services and fights the IDF. Though the leaders remain very local and parochial in their outlook, they are learning. "The leadership could use six weeks in New York," Omar says. "They need to learn more about the outside world."

Back at the hotel, we hear a commotion in the lobby and go to investigate. To the sound of drums and musical pipes, a wedding party enters. The men dance in circles around the groom, singing and jumping. The bride follows on her father's arm. She is wearing a long white gown and veil and carrying a huge bunch of white flowers. The joyous scene provides a stark contrast to what we have otherwise witnessed on this long day.

Khan Younis City

June 3

We're up for a speed walk at seven a.m., much to the alarm of the UN and Hamas security guards. They are concerned about our possible abduction by "extremists" or Mossad agents. A guard with an AK-47 tries to keep up but can't. We tell him not to worry and finish our walk. The streets are clean but there are few cars. Many donkey carts are driven by middle-class people. A water truck goes by, and the driver waves.

Extensive bombing eliminated many factories in Khan Younis City. Those spared are nevertheless nonfunctional for lack of materials and parts.

At the Khan Younis Club, boys and girls under the age of twelve learn dance, gymnastics, and music. We sit outside under a shade tree in a circle to talk with the director. She can barely contain her anger. "Other delegations have come and gone but nothing is done," she says. "The children have nightmares. They paint pictures of war, they become violent. The Israelis should be tried as war criminals. Palestinians have the right to resist. The Israelis destroy life in many ways. Khan Younis was an IDF military base, and, for fifteen years, Gazans could not go to their own beach."

Her brother, an ambulance driver, was killed in the Israeli raids. We tell her that Medea and Tighe are going to Cairo to try to persuade Obama to come to Gaza or to send a representative. She nods without expression, looking down at the ground.

A few meters away, a dozen young boys are doing somersaults under the supervision of a bearded coach. They run, flip, and land on their feet, over and over, until the youngest can do it.

A group of about twelve students at the Khan Younis Training Center have built an automobile from scratch in hopes of entering an international competition somewhere in Europe. They have used parts cannibalized from junked Fiats. However, their dream has little chance of fulfillment. They will not be allowed to leave Gaza. And even here, their chances of employment are slim. Still, they pose by the welded skeleton, smiling. They've done this to show they can.

Sinai, Cairo

June 4

It is my birthday. We drive back to the Rafah crossing.

There is a farewell demonstration. We unfurl banners calling on Obama to visit Gaza. The Mayor of Rafah, Gaza, thanks us profusely, and a few of us give speeches.

The most touching remarks come from the family that housed Rachel Corrie, a college student from Washington State who had come to Gaza in 2003 and worked with the ISM. She was killed when she stood in front of an Israeli bulldozer as it demolished the homes of Gazans suspected of having a family member sympathetic to Hamas. "She died defending our home," says the father. "I saw them take her tiny body out of the rubble. We will never forget her."

Their home was demolished despite Rachel's sacrifice.

The buses are delayed at the border again. We figure the Egyptians want to make sure that Obama and his entourage are safely out of Cairo before they send two busloads of pro-Palestinian activists there. Finally, in the late afternoon, the Egyptians get the word. In a big hurry now, they distribute our passports, load our luggage, collect another entrance fee, and practically push us through the gates. Again, we are escorted by security vehicles with teenage soldiers sitting in the back of pickups, holding the ever-present AK-47s. Every now and then, a black Mercedes pulls alongside the bus, and a security honcho admonishes the bus driver to go faster. People smile and wave and give us the "V" sign. In the bus, we sing.

The sun sets on the barren but beautiful Sinai landscape. Norm points and says to me, "That's your birthday card."

Finally, the buses stop in front of the Pension Roma, where it all began. We are incredibly tired but indelibly changed, and irrevocably committed.

Epilogue

At the request of Israel, Egypt has closed the Rafah border crossing to anyone sympathetic to the Palestinian cause.

On June 8, 2014, the IDF launched Operation Protective Edge. The damage to Palestinian life and property was even greater than that inflicted during Operation Cast Lead. Israel's blockade of Gaza remains in effect.

Although many American politicians have visited Israel, no one, including Obama, has gone to Gaza.

Back in Brooklyn, we host two events in our apartment to publicize the plight of Gaza's population: one to provide an informational session and one to raise funds. People are sympathetic—they pay attention and give money—but then go on with their lives. We attend marches and rallies, some in front of the Israeli Consulate in New York, to protest the blockade and also Benjamin Netanyahu's policy of displacing Palestinians to build settlements for Israelis. Netanyahu just builds more settlements.

We protest the firing or demotions of academics who criticize Israeli policies toward the Palestinians. Some professors are reinstated, others receive settlements, and the rest move on. We participate in a movement to boycott Israeli products at our Food Co-op in Brooklyn, an attempt that triggers hysterical and hostile reactions from the opposition. Two thousand people assemble to vote for or against conducting a referendum on the boycott, standing room only in the largest high school auditorium in Brooklyn. The pro-referendum position gets forty percent of the total, a showing that would have been unheard of five years earlier.

We are not discouraged. All of these actions have educated the American public about a situation that is not given much attention in the mainstream media. And young people, on college campuses and everywhere else, including in the Park Slope Food Co-op, are actively supporting the Palestinian cause.

There is hope for the future.

Ethiopia:

THE OMO RIVER VALLEY

Hamer Bull-Jumping Ceremony

We stand in the glare of the south Ethiopian sun. A cloud of ochre dust leaves a fine powder that turns dark red in the rivulets of our sweat. Our water bottles are almost empty, and the remaining liquid is dishpan warm. We accept this discomfort for the chance to witness the bull-jumping ceremony of a traditional Hamer village in the Lower Omo River Valley.

As part of their initiation into manhood, young Hamer men, aged fourteen to eighteen years old, are required to jump on and run across the backs of a line of bulls, making this traverse several times without falling. Much celebration precedes the initiate's athletic feat, and, if he is successful, his village feasts for two days. If not, he is shamed until his next try.

The event takes place on the Ethiopian savanna in an unnamed village near the town of Turmi, where we had spent the night. To reach the village, our Toyota 4x4 rumbles over dubious roads for two hours, slewing and swerving up a dry riverbed filled with sand until it can go no further. Then our guide, G. Hiwot Chemdessa ("call me

G"), spends half an hour negotiating an "entry" fee with the village chief, a stubborn old man with a fixed scowl.

Money paid, we hike through sand piles toward a cacophony of sound: drums beating; horns blowing; rattles shaking; and singing, chanting, shouting, and ululating. The noise is coming from a large clearing bordered by acacia trees and thorn bushes. A phalanx of women, teens to crones, is doing a shuffling, arm-waving, hip-shaking slow march around the field, raising dust as they go. Every few minutes, they stop and jump up and down in unison, alternating high and low jumps, shouting as they do. They then resume their rhythmic progress.

The women combine complex hair weaves with decorative head shaving and a binding mix of ochre and water to achieve shiny copper braids, each displaying her own unique hairstyle. They wear animal skins decorated with intricate beadwork; cowrie shell necklaces; silver rattles on their ankles; scrap wire wound decoratively around their wrists, upper arms, and necks; and beaded headbands secured with white feathers. Their faces are painted, mostly with slashes of red and yellow. The men dress in a similar, but more restrained, fashion.

The Hamer are high on homemade beer. Some sleep in the scant shade of an acacia, using small carved wooden saddle-shaped headrests that also function as stools. Others, sitting or standing, lean against the skinny tree trunks and shout comments to their friends or to the dancers.

Strange and disturbing enactments occur in the brush bordering the field. To show their love for the initiate, his close female relatives and friends challenge men of the village to hit them across their bare lower backs with switches. The logic of this painful display escapes us, but the passion of the participants does not. I watch two young women fight over a switch to determine whom will be hit first. The blows must be sharp enough to draw blood, or the man wielding the switch is loudly taunted by the women, who bear thick scars from prior ceremonies.

Another dust cloud blooms in the distance. Men are driving bulls toward the ceremonial field. The dancers are nearing ecstasy, jumping higher and shouting louder. Two hundred Hamer and a scattering of tourists gather around the bulls as they arrive. Tribal elders wade into the herd to pick candidates for the lineup.

The initiate appears. But for a small skin vest, he is naked. He is tall, over six feet, wiry, dust-covered, and shaved bald except for the back of his head where his hair grows in frizzy profusion. He looks a little long in the tooth to be under eighteen. He is calm and focused, his brow furrowed. He, too, wades into the herd. He is allowed to pick out one of the bulls for the jump. We speculate it is not his first try. This village is taking no chances; nobody wants an otherwise healthy bachelor hanging around his parents' hut and eating their provender indefinitely.

The chanting and shouting suddenly stops. The chosen bulls, bawling and eyes rolling in fear, are lined up, side by side, and held in place, each by one man holding its upper jaw and another holding its tail. There are two small bulls on the outside and three large bulls in the center.

The youth takes a short run-up, jumps on the back of one of the small bulls, steps up and onto the three big bulls, jumps down to the other small bull, and then down to the ground. He turns and does the same thing five more times, without a stumble, slip, or hesitation. He has been practicing.

Strangely enough, there is no cheering, noisemaking, or rush to congratulate him or his family. The Hamer, tired and relieved, straggle off to their huts to begin two days of serious partying. The initiate will receive a small starter herd from the village, enabling him to begin his adult life as putative husband, herdsman, and warrior.

Bull jumper, Hamer village

Bull-jumping celebrant, Hamer village

I think about the meaning of this ritual. The Hamer are subsistence agro-pastoralists. While they grow crops, their significant possession is the cattle herd, whose size determines the prestige of the owner. This ceremony symbolizes the intimate relationship between the Hamer and their cattle and their benign but firm control over the herd.

We are in the center of the Omo River Valley in southern Ethiopia, an area that is a crazy quilt of tribes with different cultures living in close, though not always peaceful, contact with one another. Most are pastoral, engaging, if at all, in minimal subsistence farming. Ownership of cattle is the measure of wealth. There occur, therefore, frequent clashes between the tribes over allegations of cattle rustling, leading to armed combat and some fatalities.

There is also a problem with banditry in the Valley involving attacks on passing vehicles. The Ethiopian government requires that an armed escort accompany tourists. For much of our three-week stay, Barbara and I are crammed into a Toyota Land Cruiser with our guide, our driver, and an armed uniformed militiaman.

Hair, Termites, and Bananas

Hair is very important throughout the Omo Valley. Men and women spend hours grooming their own and each other's hair, plaiting, twisting, cornrowing, or coloring and sometimes all four at once. Or the hair is shaved into intricate designs on the scalp, or the front of the hairline is trimmed back, displaying a large forehead. We brought straight razors as gifts to be used for that purpose, and they were much appreciated.

Each tribe has its own unique style. Within that parameter, individuals create their own approach. In some areas, certain styles and colors are relegated to unmarried women, making it easy for the men to decide with whom to flirt. By adding beads to hair as well as putting on different bracelets, anklets, necklaces, and clothes, the possibilities are endless.

A much less attractive feature of Omo Valley life are the termites, with whom the villagers live side by side. The termites flourish, creating hundreds of rust-colored towers, some over twelve feet tall. The towers are impermeable, protected by a hard crust, standing straight up from the dry savannah like so many stupas in the Burmese plain. Although purportedly beneficial to agriculture because of the fertile soil they create out of woody fiber, they are mostly destructive, decimating houses and crops.

The Dorze tribe has found a way to live with them. They build conical houses, at least twenty feet tall, with a high entrance opening and vestibule, although the people are of average height. At first, we wonder why they went to so much trouble to build such towering structures, graceful as they appear—the reason is that the termites eat the wooden base from the bottom, slowly shortening the house to a "normal" size. The houses are also built to be portable, allowing the Dorze to move them off the damaged foundation. By planning ahead, they can live in the same house for at least one or two generations.

Bananas also loom large in Ethiopian economy and culture. There are, of course, the plain-eating, true bananas, which are grown for home use, local markets,

Dorze house

and export. Ethiopia grows a variety of bananas for consumption, including tiny three-to-four-inch ones that are especially big on flavor.

More important to the community is the false banana, a plant that looks very similar to a young true banana tree but bears no edible fruit. Its leaves are used as roof shingles throughout the country. It also serves as animal fodder and, with effort, can be made edible for humans, providing a substitute for *injira*, the ubiquitous Ethiopian flatbread. The false banana is indigenous to Ethiopia, where it is cultivated in addition to being gathered in the wild.

And then there is "banana art," invented by a Rastafarian named Bandi who operates the Banana Art Gallery in a large Rastafarian community near Addis Ababa. He is very handsome, with gray hair in Rasta braids, a mustache, and a short beard on an unlined face. Originally from Saint Vincent, he explains what he does in his musical Caribbean English and shows us his press clippings and his degree from the Royal Academy of Art in London. Bandi creates collages made up of material from dried true and false banana plants. His work depicts scenes from village life and ranges from large, framed pieces to greeting cards. We purchase some cards before we leave.

Thousands of Rastafarians from the Caribbean now live in Ethiopia because they worship Haile Selassie, who ruled Ethiopia as Emperor from 1930 to 1974. On two different occasions, major droughts ended immediately after Selassie visited Jamaica, and he is now revered as the Messiah.

The Surmi

The towns in the deep south near the Kenyan border bristle with automatic weapons. Kibbish is in the middle of the area occupied by the Surmi, a tall, slender, handsome people. They walk slowly along the roads with long, loping strides. Both men and women wear a large piece of woven green fabric over one shoulder, covering their torso down to midcalf. Almost all the men carry an AK-47. The Surmi herd cattle and do a little farming.

The Surmi women are known for the holes in their lower lips into which they insert objects the size of small plates. They start with a small pierced hole and place successively larger discs in the space, gradually stretching the skin. They follow the same procedure in their earlobes. A few of the men have stretched earlobes, and even fewer have an expanded lower lip. It appears grotesque to us, but what is important is that it is a standard of beauty for the Surmi. They have altered their faces and ears in this way for centuries. Now, physical alterations based on tradition have turned into a money-making venture, attracting tourists who pay for photo opportunities.

G says the men go into town and get drunk every night. In the late afternoon, it is the women's turn. Sitting at a small café on a dusty side street in Kibbish, we observe Surmi women crowding into a tiny bar. Loud fights break out and spill onto the street. Eventually, the barkeep comes outside to restrain the combatants, and all is calm until the next dispute.

The next morning, we go to a Surmi village. The faces of the women and children are painted with circles and dots, white against their dark skin. Each design is unique. One man has decorated half of his face with white paint and wears curved animal horns above his ears. The villagers dance and sing, and it's obvious that they have already dipped into their homemade beer.

G, a Hamer, says that the Surmi are not trusted by other tribes, that they are cattle thieves, and that they don't even trust one another, concealing their cattle from other tribal members. I wonder what the Surmi have to say about the Hamer, but we don't know for sure. Everywhere else we went, we were welcomed with coffee, tea, or homemade brew, even when we dropped in unannounced. Not so with the Surmi.

The *Burji* of the Dizi

The Dizi people live in the hill country in close proximity to the Surmi. The Chief, or *Burji*, oversees several villages within his jurisdiction. He has two personal compounds—one in the valley and one on a hilltop—and four wives, thirty-four children, countless grandchildren, hundreds of cattle, and one hand. He lost the other hand in a fight with Surmi cattle thieves.

We sit on the front porch of his hilltop house. It is a nontraditional rectangular affair, constructed of cement block, set on an acre of land and surrounded by a seven-foot-high bamboo fence. Little children scamper in and out of the house, sometimes stopping to receive his caresses or standing behind him to peek at us. Chickens nod and peck in the front yard. The Burji, barefoot, wearing a baseball cap, shorts, and an unbuttoned short-sleeve shirt, sits on the porch stoop. He looks to be in his late fifties or early sixties and is strong and fit. He insists that we, as his guests, occupy a bench, the only furniture available. He smiles a lot and laughs easily. Encouraged by G, he relates some of his history.

His father was killed before his eyes for refusing to cooperate with agents of the Derg, the military cabal that ran Ethiopia from 1974 to 1991. On the pretense of carrying out land redistribution, Derg officials confiscated land to enrich themselves. The Burji was arrested and tortured for trying to defend his father and refusing to sign over half of his family estate. After his release, he killed a Derg general and burned down a barracks. He fled and lived in exile in Sudan until the Derg was overthrown. He returned home a hero and the people chose him as Burji, rejecting his older brother who had not put up any resistance to the Derg.

The Burji thinks of himself not as a chief but as a farmer. He has won several awards from the government as an agronomist and shows us the certificates. The villagers have adopted his farming

techniques, including terracing, much to their benefit. He has jurisdiction to adjudge minor domestic, property, and criminal disputes.
When we ask how he resolves conflicts between his constituents, he
says that there are none because he knows everybody, visits all the
villages monthly, and heads off any trouble he thinks is brewing.

The Burji asks if we would like a drink of homemade liquor. Then,
he comments that he would like to have a foreign wife and offers one
hundred cattle for Barbara. Startled, we laugh, and he doesn't press the
matter. I tell him, "Be careful what you wish for." He laughs, disappears
into the house and emerges with a bottle and some shot glasses. The
liquor has a nice vodka taste, but it goes down like liquid fire.

He takes us on a tour along a path that skirts fields of corn and
makes its way along a fence line downhill into the valley of a stream. The
air is cooler and there is shade from various fruit trees. We come to a
compound of several traditional round, thatched mud huts, each about
six meters in diameter, occupied by his wives, children, and grandchildren. They emerge, smiling, to welcome him. Other relatives drift into
the compound. Soon there are thirty adults and many children milling

The Burji of the Dizi and one of his wives, Ethiopia

about, gossiping, greeting us, posing for Barbara's camera, and laughing at the results. With the assistance of wife number one, everyone is herded into a group, and Barbara takes the family picture.

We set up our tents in the front yard of an abandoned school down the road from the Burji's hilltop compound. Up to this point, I haven't seen any weapons, but that night the Burji posts two armed guards at the entrance to the schoolyard.

Early in the morning, we are ready to move on but do not want to leave without saying good-bye. The Burji's grandchildren run to get him from the fields, where he is working, and he arrives, sweating, machete under his arm, very pleased that we waited for him to say farewell.

The *Abageda*

We visit a village of the Boreno people, a large tribe of mostly Muslims scattered in a thousand small villages near the Kenyan and Sudanese borders. The village is surrounded by termite towers taller than their huts. By chance, a postmeeting party of local chiefs is taking place in one of the huts, and we are invited in to meet them. A dozen men, along with the woman whose hut they are occupying, relax with a few beers. They have just met with the *Abageda* (or chief of chiefs) to discuss agricultural issues and relations between the Boreno and Kenya and Sudan.

The Abageda is chosen by the village chiefs and serves an eight-year term, but he can be removed if he is not doing his job. The tribe has a two-court judicial system: a court of elders who mete out justice in numbers of cows to be paid and a government civil court. The Abageda goes barefoot, even to international conferences. He has a car for official travel but prefers to ride a horse.

With their permission, Barbara takes pictures. They hide their beer bottles just before she trips the shutter.

205

Timkat in Arba Minch

Forty-four percent of Ethiopia's population is Orthodox Christian. Thirty-four percent are Muslim. Most of the rest are animists. Ethiopia was the second country (after Armenia) to adopt Christianity as the state religion. The Christian population controls a disproportionate share of the state's government, economy, and culture. Their language, Amharic, is the official language of Ethiopia, and it is taught in all the schools. The Christians are concentrated in the central highlands and Addis Ababa, but even in the Omo Valley there are cities like Arba Minch, with a population of ninety-five thousand, that are almost wholly Christian. And it seems like all ninety-five thousand are in the streets to celebrate the holy day of Timkat, the day Jesus was baptized by John.

The ceremonies start in the Cathedral of St. Gabriel with the bishop intoning chants a thousand years old, amplified for the crowd outside. After about an hour, he emerges, chanting and carrying a silver ciborium containing a relic, probably the bone of a saint or a piece of the true cross. He wears a dark-red miter topped with what looks like a large, flat, square-shaped pillow, black with a gold fringe. From this pillow hangs heavy red cloth, lined with orange, which covers the side of the bishop's face and his shoulders down to his waist. All—miter, pillow, and red fabric—are embroidered in elaborate patterns of gold and silver. Underneath is a heavy white robe.

The bishop is surrounded by lower-ranking clergy in similar vestments with slightly less ornamentation. One holds a white umbrella (more fringes) over the bishop's head. In turn, each has their own yellow or white umbrellas with fringes. A team of lay assistants spreads red carpets in their path, rolling up the carpet the bishop and his entourage just walked on and unrolling it and sweeping it clean in front of them again, providing a continuous cushion for the bishop's slippers. Behind the umbrella-clad clergy file members of religious associations in their traditional uniforms. Then come the most devout laypersons, the men in their best dark suits, the women wearing white shawls. Many also carry umbrellas, some white and others in bright colors.

From time to time, the procession stops altogether while the bishop chants a prayer. Teenagers break into their own chant or song, leaping together in small groups like a traveling rave party. The wide boulevard and sidewalks are filled with people from wall to wall. We walk with the faithful, attracting a lot of stares, but everyone is loose, friendly, and having a good time. The constant joyful cacophony of drums, amplified chants, cheers, songs, and ululation fills the air. We are carried along in a human flood, a torrent of ecstasy.

After about half a mile, the procession is joined by another phalanx, the congregation and clergy from St. Michael's. The swollen mass shuffles and dances toward a soccer stadium at the edge of town. Individuals and small groups begin to peel off from the crowd and make for the stadium in order to get a good seat. We follow suit.

Timkat faithful, Arba Minch

The stadium fills up quickly. Young vendors hawking souvenirs and religious pendants work the crowd. Finally, the big white umbrella comes into view, bobbing like a ship on a sea of heads. The stadium crowd cheers, but then moans as the procession turns into an adjoining field.

Most of the stadium faithful start to leave, as do we. Having guessed wrongly on the procession's destination, by the time they could get to the other field they would be too far away for a good view of the holy rites. In the other field, the bishop begins what will be twenty-four hours of standing and constant prayer.

Perhaps we should have paid more attention to the bishop's prayers. A day after we leave Arba Minch, I come down with a serious intestinal disorder. The next day, Barbara gets sick. We have ImmodiumD but it doesn't faze the bug—and we forgot to bring Cipro. Fortunately for us, the Ethiopian government has established a network of rural clinics staffed by doctors who have agreed to work in these facilities for five years in return for free medical education. By late afternoon, G is knocking on the door of the doctor's small residence while we wait in the 4x4, sick as dogs. She is preparing dinner but puts it aside and goes right to work. She provides a supply of Cipro and gives us IVs to replace the nutrients we have lost. Things get better right away, and we're able to resume the trip.

Many in remote villages still rely on traditional medicine men (who are all men) for remedies. We observe an eighty-five-year-old man as he ministers to people in his "clinic," a small central square in an isolated village, using herbs he gathers in the forest. Sometimes he disappears for days to search for the plants he needs. He claims to have healed broken bones, eased a difficult childbirth, relieved headaches, straightened and strengthened a sore back, and eliminated a fungus. His eldest son is learning his secrets and will succeed him.

Fidel Slept Here

The Bebeka coffee and tea plantation is Africa's oldest and one of the world's largest. It is in fact a small town with forty thousand residents, twenty thousand of whom work in its fields. Amid the coffee and tea plants is a community center with an area set aside for camping, which we plan to use.

The grounds are beautifully kept. There is a sense of peace in the deep shade. That is, until two busloads of raucous, energized young people, dressed in their best clothes, unload at the gate. A wedding party has come to take photos with the lush foliage as background. The principals are in full regalia. The bride wears a long white dress and veil, and the maids of honor are in turquoise. The men sport dark suits. A professional photographer rallies them around. So, of course, Barbara unlimbers her Canon, gives everybody a smile and a handshake, and gets permission to take her own photos. An hour and one hundred photo opportunities later, the youngsters pile into their buses and wave good-bye.

We are getting ready to set up camp when G brings news. There are two cabins on the property for special guests that are not currently in use, so the manager, in deference to our gray hair, has offered them to us and G. We gratefully accept. The "cabins" are Craftsman-style bungalows, the interiors of which are larger than our apartment in New York, and the stone and concrete exteriors look like they could take a direct hit from a tank shell and not be any the worse for it.

We learn that the bungalow in which we are to stay was occupied five times by Fidel Castro when he attended Third World conferences in Addis Ababa. We sleep comfortably in Fidel's bedstead.

The Dig

On our last day in the Valley, we visit the Melka Kunture Prehistoric Site, a round dig about six meters in diameter and two meters deep, sheltered by a peaked roof and open at the sides. The site is supervised by a lone doctoral student who gives us a tour. A nearby museum contains artifacts found during the dig.

The site has been virtually abandoned for several years. What is special about this project, according to the young guide, is that the archeologists found stone and obsidian tools and chip marks on bones of animals, providing evidence of human habitation. Experts have concluded that, based on their placement in the rock strata, these artifacts and bones are more than one million years old. In 1974, a team of archeologists working near the Awash River in Ethiopia found the skeleton of a female, subsequently named "Lucy." The remains, estimated to be 3.2 million years old, were at the time the oldest evidence of bipedal hominins who had stood upright and walked erect. A 4.4-million-year-old specimen was later found in the same area, giving Ethiopia a claim to being the cradle of humanity.

A touching find at the Melka Kunture Prehistoric Site is the footprints, preserved in stone, of what is assumed to be a mother and child. The adult's steps appear to be closely spaced so as to match those of the child.

The most important pieces are locked in glass cases. However, there are also stone hand tools and spherical stone balls used in cooking that visitors can pick up and handle, which I do. I am moved by this contact, however remote, with a human like myself, who was beginning to think, learn, and teach—the start of the long climb up the ladder of evolution and adaptation to dominance over the planet and all species, for better or for worse.

We ask the young student about his future. He shrugs his shoulders. "There are no jobs for archeologists in Ethiopia," he says. "The government is not interested."

Epilogue

On August 21, 2016, Feyisa Lilesa raises his arms and crosses them in an "X" as he reaches the finish line to win the silver medal in the Olympic marathon event, calling the world's attention to antigovernment protests taking place in Ethiopia, where people have taken to the streets to demand political change.

The Oromos and Amharas, the two largest ethnic groups in the country, feel marginalized by the Tigrayan ethnic group, which constitutes only 6 percent of the population but controls the government, the military, intelligence services, and commerce. The government brutally represses any opposition. Despite being an Olympic hero, Lilesa is afraid to return to his home and is worried about his family's safety.

Afterword

What have we gained from sitting in a climate-controlled tube for hours on end to get to places where we must hike up and down steep trails in the tropical sun or freezing cold; slog through mud or dust; eat strange food; fall sick; get bitten by mosquitoes and ants; set up tents on rooftops, in parking lots, or on grass littered with yak dung; and sleep in places with no toilet or shower facilities?

A lot. We have seen many beautiful sights—mountains, rivers, art, architecture, monuments—but have enjoyed and learned most from our interactions with individuals and families. People we met, no matter what their tribe, clan, religion, country of origin or residence, color, political beliefs, or role in the family or community want the same thing: peace, a home, and a way to put food on the table. They also want something to sustain their spirits: art, music, dance, literature, and the right to a belief system, whether political, religious, or spiritual. Most of all, they want to control their own lives and provide for their children.

But increasingly, given the global economic and political situation, such control is being eroded. The ways of life of indigenous peoples in Papua New Guinea, Cameroon, Ethiopia, and on the Orinoco are threatened by commercial interests and complicit governments. Political events are undermining the lives of people in Venezuela. In Gaza, Palestinians live under the constant threat of bombardment.

Nepal is in turmoil because of natural disasters and unstable govern-ments. We don't know whether the lives of Iranians or Cubans will improve with the lifting of sanctions and the end of the embargo.

And yet, the people we visited, even in places considered unsafe by the State Department, were friendly and hospitable. Sometimes those who had the least material wealth gave us the most—not only food and gifts such as shell necklaces and carved walking sticks, but also smiles and hugs. They were proud to share their lives and cul-ture with us. They let us participate in their celebrations. They will-ingly posed for photographs because it made them laugh, and they saw that it made us happy.

Our guides, with rare exception, were excellent—knowledgea-ble and kind. Most became guides because they could not find other work—as teachers, craftsmen, skilled workers, or businessmen—to support their families. We learned about their lives, families, and dreams—and they about ours.

After we left, disaster, natural or man-made, hit several of the countries we visited. We are concerned about the people we left behind. We were able to communicate with some of the guides via email, but now most of our inquiries go unanswered. We have no idea what has happened to them.

There is a bright spot. We did not travel to the far northern areas of Cameroon because Boko Haram, a jihadist group, was mak-ing incursions, kidnapping people, and destroying villages. This situ-ation has since become much more dangerous. Jones, our guide, was a dealer in artifacts and a source of information about the wonders of African art. He was also sensitive to our interests, modifying our plans to show us something he thought we would want to see—and he would always be right. In one of the memorable detours, he took us to his home, where we had a delicious lunch with his family. When I was dehydrated and had to spend the night in a hospital in a rural area, he refused to go back to the hotel and slept in the car. "In case you need me," he said.

Jones's wife was studying in San Antonio, Texas, while we were in Cameroon. He was waiting for a visa to come to the US with their young daughter. Knowing the reluctance with which our government issues visas and the looming danger from Boko Haram in Cameroon, we recently emailed him to ask where he is now. The news is good. He and his daughter are in Texas with his wife and their two sons. Jones has found some work, although it has been a difficult, and is continuing his struggle to adjust. But he and his family are together, and they are safe.

We wish the same for everyone: in all the countries we have visited, in all the countries yet to come, and everywhere in the world.

Next trip: Angola.

Dennis James, 2016

Acknowledgments

We would like to thank everyone who offered the help and encouragement without which this book would never have been written.

Martha Hughes, the leader of my longtime writing group, was the best teacher, promoter, and supporter one could wish for. The other members of the group, Maureen Johnson-Laird, Doug Wingo, Lisa Wohl, Keith McDermott, and Joe Levine, provided valuable and constructive criticism as well. To all of them, we will continue to repay in kind.

Our agent, Priya Doraswamy, was always cheerful and indefatigable in her advocacy on our behalf. Our editor, Kim Lim, has been reasonable and accommodating. We consider ourselves lucky to have been able to work with both of them.

We have received expert technical assistance, particularly with the photographs, from Thomas Fichter, a truly professional photographer, and especially from our grandchildren, Elana and Benjamin Sewell-Grossman. We are most grateful for their help. They saved us from many wasted hours and a great deal of stress.

Finally, a big thank-you to our children, Elizabeth, Jonathan, Kiley, and Maya, for putting up with our travel dreams, despite their worries. The best thing about traveling was knowing that we would come home to you.